THE OLD VIC

FUTURE CONDITIONAL

1 SEP - 3 OCT 2015

THE HAIRY APE

17 OCT - 21 NOV 2015

By EUGENE O'NEILL

DR. SEUSS'S THE LORAX

3 DEC 2015 - 16 JAN 2016

Adapted by DAVID GREIG

PRINCIPAL PARTNER ROYAL BANK OF CANADA

THE MASTER BUILDER

By HENRIK IBSEN
New adaptation by DAVID HARE

23 JAN - 19 MAR 2016

THE McONIE COMPANY'S

JEKYLL & HYDE

A NEW DANCE THRILLER

20-28 MAY 2016

THE CARETAKER

By HAROLD PINTER

26 MAR - 14 MAY 2016

GROUNDHOG DAY

Book by DANNY RUBIN
Music & lyrics by TIM MINCHIN

RISE

OUR COMMUNITY PRODUCTION

0844 871 7628
oldvictheatre.com

PRINCIPAL PARTNER

RBC

Royal Bank of Canada

GRANTA

12 Addison Avenue, London W11 4QR | email editorial@granta.com
To subscribe go to granta.com, or call 020 8955 7011 (free phone 0500 004 033)
in the United Kingdom, 845-267-3031 (toll-free 866-438-6150) in the United States

ISSUE 133: AUTUMN 2015

PUBLISHER AND EDITOR	Sigrid Rausing
DEPUTY EDITOR	Rosalind Porter
POETRY EDITOR	Rachael Allen
ONLINE EDITOR	Luke Neima
DESIGNER	Daniela Silva
EDITORIAL ASSISTANTS	Eleanor Chandler, Josie Mitchell, Francisco Vilhena
SUBSCRIPTIONS	David Robinson
PUBLICITY	Pru Rowlandson
TO ADVERTISE CONTACT	Kate Rochester, katerochester@granta.com
FINANCE	Morgan Graver
SALES AND MARKETING	Iain Chapple, Katie Hayward
IT MANAGER	Mark Williams
PRODUCTION ASSOCIATE	Sarah Wasley
PROOFS	Amber Dowell, Katherine Fry, Jessica Kelly, Vimbai Shire
CONTRIBUTING EDITORS	Daniel Alarcón, Anne Carson, Mohsin Hamid, Isabel Hilton, Michael Hofmann, A.M. Homes, Janet Malcolm, Adam Nicolson, Edmund White

YOU'RE NEXT

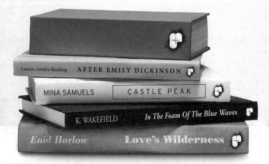

Lauren Amalia Redding — AFTER EMILY DICKINSON

MINA SAMUELS — CASTLE PEAK

K. WAKEFIELD — In The Foam Of The Blue Waves

Enid Harlow — Love's Wilderness

Publishing Fall 2015
penandbrush.org

There's a long history of writing women (*writers*) off. It's time to right that wrong.

Visit penandbrush.org to submit your literary portfolio now and you could be next.

PEN + BRUSH
Until it's just about the art

29 East 22nd Street New York, NY 10010 212-475-3669

NEW YORK, 1977

‘Over the course of Hallberg’s magisterial epic, distinctions of class, race, geography, and generation give way to an impression of the human condition that is both ambitious and sublime’

VANITY FAIR

BE THERE WHEN IT EXPLODES

WEST AFRICA
Word, Symbol, Song

Exhibition open until 16 February 2016

An exhibition of literature and music – from the great African empires of the Middle Ages to the cultural dynamism of West Africa today.

BRITISH LIBRARY

#BLwestafrica

Book now www.bl.uk

Fela Kuti by Bernard Matussière, reproduced by kind permission of Knitting Factory Records.

21 - 25 January 2016

JAIPUR LITERATURE FESTIVAL

Diggi Palace Jaipur

Attending Speakers

Alka Saraogi
Anita Nair
Anjum Hasan
Anuradha Roy
Armistead Maupin
Ayesha Jalal
Ben Macintyre
Christina Lamb
Colm Tóibín
David Grossman
James Shapiro

Margaret Atwood
Niall Ferguson
Nilanjana S. Roy
Raghu Karnad
Richard Sennett
Roberto Calasso
Sitanshu Yashaschandra
Sunjeev Sahota
Susan Abulhawa
Uday Prakash
Vivek Shanbhag
and many more...

Produced by **TEAMWORK**
CELEBRATING THE ARTS

CONTENTS

Introduction

There is an apocalyptic feeling in the air. I write the day after the news that the IS have blown up parts of the ancient site of Palmyra. They had already beheaded the eminent archaeologist Khaled al-Asaad and, according to reports, hung his body from the monuments. Refugees are drowning in the Mediterranean and living in makeshift camps at Calais and in Budapest; the Ukrainian film director Oleg Sentsov has been charged with terrorism offences by the Russian authorities in Crimea and sentenced to twenty years in prison. 'Hang on in there, Oleg,' someone writes. It's not *Darkness at Noon* but maybe it should be.

This issue began with discussions about the environment – a word that is now almost permanently linked to the idea of destruction; humanity's capacity to build and to blindly destroy. And yet there is also hope. Our opening piece, by Barry Lopez, is a profound meditation on nature observation. Lopez shows how our ambition to tell the story of what we see is often too hasty. We may overlook peripheral signs, and miss what he terms the *unfolding* of the event we are witnessing.

Adam Nicolson's piece is set in Romania, in the post-1989 world of idyllic hay meadows and apple orchards: the world we have lost in the West. But this pretty stretch of countryside is riven by murderous violence caused by ancient rivalries over land played out now in the context of the EU and depopulation. Nicolson met one of the murderers. Half his face had been destroyed by a bear, a casual clawing, the weapons at hand useless – those knives and hoes which are also tools of killing men are no good with a bear.

We may long for a natural world where children are 'free to roam', or 'free to be bored'. But remember Flaubert's description of Charles Bovary's idiotic rural upbringing – we mourn the loss of that aimless running about in the woods eating blackberries and ringing the church bells for the pleasure of dangling on the rope, but Flaubert did not: 'Madame Bovary would bite her lip, and the child was left to wander about the village.' And remember Theodor Fontane's *Effi Briest* (1894), and the curious parental concern about excessive reading in that novel. That turned into a parental concern about excessive TV, and now the Internet. We have our worries, and they had theirs – the content changes a bit, but the feeling remains the same.

In this present zeitgeist dominated by terrorists and climate change we have almost forgotten the apocalyptic fears of the past, but I grew up with the idea of nuclear extinction. Fred Pearce, in this issue, discusses the Herculean effort to keep Sellafield safe after the accident in 1957. Windscale, as it was known then, was originally a project to produce weapons material, not energy. It is a half-forgotten wasteland now, but it contains more radioactive material in so small a space than anywhere else in Europe. And it is intensely guarded, for that reason, as it will have to be for a thousand years to come.

Australian writer Rebecca Giggs witnesses the long process of a whale dying on a beach. It's a surreal and painful scene – the whale lies dying, probably sick, or poisoned by plastics or toxins. It's slowly overheating, surrounded by singing people, paying homage. There are sodden flowers, candles. We want it to be over; it takes so long.

Nothing changes in the face of extinction. Rome burns, century after century, and we fiddle, hoping for the best, turning away from the flames; staring hypnotised into the flames; throwing fuel onto the flames. And then we dust ourselves off and start again, marching towards the next catastrophe.

And yet the pleasure of reading remains. 'The text you write must prove to me *that it desires me,*' Barthes wrote about the pleasures of the text. I hope that the pleasure of being the *desired reader* might do something to alleviate the sense of doom in our title. ■

Sigrid Rausing

THE INVITATION

Barry Lopez

When I was young, and just beginning to travel with them, I imagined that indigenous people saw more and heard more, that they were overall simply more aware than I was. They were more aware, and did see and hear more than I did. The absence of spoken conversation whenever I was traveling with them, however, should have provided me with a clue about why this might be true; but it didn't, not for a while. It's this: when an observer doesn't immediately turn what his senses convey to him into language, into the vocabulary and syntactical framework we all employ when trying to define our experiences, there's a much greater opportunity for minor details, which might at first seem unimportant, to remain alive in the foreground of an impression, where, later, they might deepen the meaning of an experience.

If my companions and I, for example, encountered a grizzly bear feeding on a caribou carcass, I would tend to focus almost exclusively on the bear. My companions would focus on the part of the world of which, at that moment, the bear was only a fragment. The bear here might be compared with a bonfire, a kind of incandescence that throws light on everything around it. My companions would glance off into the outer reaches of that light, then look back to the fire, back and forth. They would repeatedly situate the smaller thing within the larger thing, back and forth. As they noticed trace odors in the air, or listened for birdsong or the sound of brittle brush rattling, they in effect extended the moment of encounter with the bear backward and forward in time. Their framework for the phenomenon, one that I might later shorten just to 'meeting the bear', was more voluminous than mine; and where my temporal boundaries for the event would normally consist of little more than the moments of the encounter itself, theirs included the time before we arrived, as well as the time after we left. For me, the bear was a noun, the subject of a sentence; for them, it was a verb, the gerund 'bearing'.

Over the years traveling cross-country with indigenous people I absorbed two lessons about how to be more fully present in an encounter with a wild animal. First, I needed to understand that I was entering the event as it was *unfolding*. It started before I arrived and would continue unfolding after I departed. Second, the event itself – let's say we didn't disturb the grizzly bear as he fed but only took in what he or she was doing and then slipped away – could not be completely defined by referring solely to the physical geography around us in those moments. For example, I might not recall something we'd all seen a half-hour before, a caribou hoof print in soft ground at the edge of a creek, say; but my companions would remember that. And a while after our encounter with the bear, say a half-mile farther on, they would notice something else – a few grizzly bear guard hairs snagged in scales of tree bark – and they would relate it to some detail they'd observed during those moments when we were watching the bear. The event I was cataloging in my mind as 'encounter with a tundra grizzly' they were experiencing as a sudden immersion in the current of a river. They were swimming in it, feeling its pull, noting the temperature of the water, the back eddies and where the side streams entered. My approach, in contrast, was mostly to take note of objects in the scene – the bear, the caribou, the tundra vegetation. A series of dots, which I would try to make sense of by connecting them all with a single line. My friends had situated themselves within a dynamic event. Also, unlike me, they felt no immediate need to resolve it into meaning. Their approach was to let it continue to unfold. To notice everything and to let whatever significance was there emerge in its own time.

The lesson to be learned here was not just for me to pay closer attention to what was going on around me, if I hoped to have a deeper understanding of the event, but to remain in a state of suspended mental analysis while observing all that was happening – resisting the urge to define or summarize. To step away from the familiar compulsion to understand. Further, I had to incorporate a quintessential characteristic of the way indigenous people observe: they pay more attention to *patterns* in what they encounter than to isolated objects. When they saw the bear they right away began searching for a pattern that was resolving itself before them as 'a bear feeding on a carcass'. They began gathering various pieces together that might later self-assemble into an event larger than 'a bear feeding'. These unintegrated pieces they took in as we traveled – the nature of the sonic landscape that permeated this particular physical landscape; the presence or absence of wind, and the direction from which it was coming or had shifted; a piece of speckled eggshell under a tree; leaves missing from the stems of a species of brush; a hole freshly dug in the ground – might individually convey very little. Allowed to slowly resolve into a pattern, however, they might become revelatory. They might illuminate the land further.

If the first lesson in learning how to see more deeply into a landscape was to be continuously attentive, and to stifle the urge to stand *outside* the event, to instead stay *within* the event, leaving its significance to be resolved later; the second lesson, for me, was to notice how often I asked my body to defer to the dictates of my mind, how my body's extraordinary ability to discern textures and perfumes, to discriminate among tones and colors in the world outside itself, was dismissed by the rational mind.

As much as I believed I was fully present in the physical worlds I was traveling through, I understood over time that I was not. More often I was only *thinking* about the place I was in. Initially awed by an event, the screech of a gray fox in the night woods, say, or the surfacing of a large whale, I too often moved straight to analysis. On occasion I would become so wedded to my thoughts, to some cascade of ideas, that I actually lost touch with the details that my body was *still gathering* from a place. The ear heard the song of a vesper sparrow, and then heard the song again, and knew that the second time it was a different vesper sparrow singing. The mind, pleased with itself for identifying those notes as the song of a vesper sparrow, was too preoccupied with its summary to notice what the ear was still offering. The mind was making no use of the body's ability to be discerning about sounds. And so the mind's knowledge of the place remained superficial.

Many people have written about how, generally speaking, indigenous people seem to pick up more information traversing a landscape than an outsider, someone from a culture that no longer highly values physical intimacy with a place, that regards this sort of sensitivity as a 'primitive' attribute, something a visitor from an 'advanced' culture would be comfortable believing he had actually outgrown. Such a dismissive view, as I have come to understand it, ignores the great intangible value that achieving physical intimacy with a place might provide. I'm inclined to point out to someone who condescends to such a desire for intimacy, although it might seem rude, that it is not possible for human beings to outgrow loneliness. Nor can someone from a culture that condescends to nature easily escape the haunting thought that one's life is meaningless.

Existential loneliness and a sense that one's life is inconsequential, both of which are hallmarks of modern civilizations, seem to me to derive in part from our abandoning a belief in the therapeutic dimensions of a relationship with place. A continually refreshed sense of the unplumbable complexity of patterns in the natural world, patterns that are ever present and discernible, and which incorporate the observer, undermine the feeling that one is alone in the world, or meaningless in it. The effort to know a place deeply is, ultimately, an expression of the human desire to belong, to fit somewhere.

The determination to know a particular place, in my experience, is consistently rewarded. And every natural place, to my mind, is open to being known. And somewhere in this process a person begins to sense that they *themselves* are becoming known, so that when they are absent from that place they know that place misses them. And this reciprocity, to know and be known, reinforces a sense that one is necessary in the world.

Perhaps the first rule of everything we endeavor to do is to pay attention. Perhaps the second is to be patient. And perhaps a third is to be attentive to what the body knows. In my experience, individual indigenous people are not necessarily more aware than people who've grown up in the modern culture I grew up in. Indigenous cultures, of course, are as replete with inattentive, lazy, and undiscerning individuals as 'advanced' cultures. But they tend to value more highly the importance of intimacy with a place. When you travel with them, you're acutely aware that theirs is a fundamentally different praxis from your own. They're more attentive, more patient, less willing to say what they know, to collapse mystery into language. When I was young, and one of my traveling companions would make some stunningly insightful remark about the place we were traveling through, I would sometimes feel envious; a feeling related not so much to a desire to possess that same depth of knowledge but a desire to so obviously *belong* to a particular place. To so clearly be an integral part of the place one is standing in.

A grizzly bear stripping fruit from blackberry vines in a thicket is more than a bear stripping fruit from blackberry vines in a thicket. It is a point of entry into a world most of us have turned our backs on in an effort to go somewhere else, believing we'll be better off just *thinking* about a grizzly bear stripping fruit from blackberry vines in a thicket.

The moment is an invitation, and the bear's invitation to participate is offered, without prejudice, to anyone passing by. ∎

GEORGE AND ELIZABETH

Ben Marcus

When George's father died, he neglected to tell his therapist, which wouldn't have been such a big deal, except she could cop a mood, and she knew how to punish him with a vicious show of boredom.

He'd been deep in a session with her, maintaining that when he was younger he had discovered that there was no difference, in bed, between men and women. Literally. At the biological level. If you could wrap a present, you could make one into the other. And therefore this issue of preference had weirdly become moot. You didn't have to check either box.

'Have you ever worked with clay?' he asked her. 'Have you ever pushed pudding around in your bowl?'

George gestured to show what he meant. Spoon work, a bit of charade knitting.

Dr Graco waved for him to get on with it.

It was finally, he explained, just a shame that there were no other categories he could sample.

'So you feel incapable of surprise at the sexual level?' she asked.

'I'm sure there are things out there I haven't tried, but in the end they belong to categories that have washed out for me. Just, you know, haircuts I've already had, beards I've already worn. There's too much time left on the clock. I wish that I had paced myself.'

'Paced yourself?'

'Yeah.'

'Is it a race?'

'Yes. I just got my number. I should have pinned it to my shirt. Sorry about that.'

'You don't take this seriously, do you?'

'Well . . . I pay you to take it seriously. Which gives me room to deflect and joke about it and put my insecurities on display, which you should know how to decode and use in your treatment. Another layer of evidence for your salt box.'

'Do you often think about how I conduct your treatment, as you call it?'

George sighed.

'I thought about it once, and then I died,' he said. 'I bled out.'

And boom, the session was over. He was in the waiting room putting on his coat before he remembered his news, what he'd been so determined to tell her, but he had to deal with the ovoid white-noise machine which turned speech into mush, and the miserable young man waiting his turn who refused to ever acknowledge George when he burst out of his appointment. It was all a bit exhausting. Were the two of them really supposed to pretend that they weren't both paying Dr Graco to inhale their misery and exhibit a professional silence about it? And couldn't they finally just unite in shame and even go sadly rut somewhere? Roll out their crusts against a building, even, or on the merry-go-round in Central Park?

Sex with sad people was something that could still deliver – in terms of sheer lethargy and awkwardness – but the demographics were stubborn. These people didn't exactly come out to play very often. It wasn't clear what bird call you were supposed to use. You practically had to go around knocking on doors. And then the whole thing could verge on coercion.

The news of his father's death had come in yesterday from a laundromat. Or perhaps it was simply a place with loud machines and yelling in the background. Someone was on the other end of the phone asking if a Mr George was next of kin.

At first George was confused. 'To what?' he asked. The word 'kin' made him picture the Hare Krishna display, human beings going hairless and sleek as they evolved. As if a bald, aquiline man couldn't swing a club and crush someone.

'All the tenants do a next of kin. I just need to know if that's you. Tenant name is . . . I can't really read this writing, to be honest. I didn't know this man. We have a lot of units.'

George very slowly said his father's name.

'That's it. Check. And are you Mr George?'

George said he was. Whenever someone tried to pronounce his true last name, it sounded unspeakably vulgar.

'I'm sorry to report your loss,' the voice said.

Try not to report it to too many people, George thought. Cocksucker.

He guessed he'd known he'd get a call like this one day, and he guessed he'd have to think about it for a while, because the initial impact felt mild, even irritating. He'd have to stick his head into the dirty, hot, self-satisfied state of California and try not to drown in smugness while he solved the problem of his father's body, which he hadn't particularly cared for when his father was alive. But what was most on his mind was this question of kin, and why they had not made another call first.

There was a sister, but she'd scored out of the family. It was hard to blame her. Better food, prettier people, sleeker interiors. George read about her now and then online. She'd achieved a kind of fame in the world of industrial materials. At some point she'd promoted her ridiculous middle name, Pattern, to pole position. Like Onan, maybe. Or Pelé. Her old name, Elizabeth, George figured, was holding her back, and in a way he couldn't blame her, given the sheepish Elizabeths he'd privately failed to grant human status in college. Sleepwalkers, enablers, preposterously loyal friends. Pattern was a family name belonging to their great-grandmother, who lived on a brutally cold little island, and who, according to their mother, had made a sport of surviving terminal illnesses. Now George's lovely sister Pattern, so many years later, was a person, a business, a philosophy, a crime. She did something in aerospace. Or to it. Had his brilliant sister once said, in a *Newsweek* profile, that she wanted to 'help people forget everything they thought they knew about the earth'? One such bit of hypnosis had apparently resulted in immense profits for her, the kind of money you could get very paranoid about losing. She produced shimmering synthetic materials from terribly scarce natural resources – a kind of metal drapery that served as 'towels' for drones – which meant Pattern was often photographed shaking hands with old people in robes on the tarmacs of the world, no doubt after administering shuddering handjobs to them back on the Airbus.

Well that wasn't fair. Probably, George figured, her staff conducted proclivity research so that it could provide bespoke orgasms to these titans of industry, whose children Pattern was boiling down for parts, whose reefs, mines, and caves her company was thoroughly hosing.

At home Pattern was probably submissive to a much older spouse, whose approach to gender was seasonal. Or maybe his sister wasn't married? It was difficult to remember, really. Perhaps because he had probably never known? Perhaps because Pattern did not exactly speak to any of the old family? Ever?

Now, with Mother in a Ball jar and Dad finally passed, George was the last man standing. Or sitting, really. Sort of slumped at home in the mouth of his old, disgusting couch. Trying to figure out his travel plans and how exactly he could get the bereavement discount for his flight. Like what if they tested him at the gate with their grief wand and found out, with digital certainty, that he super sort of didn't give a shit?

His most recent contact with his sister was an email from soldier1@pattern.com, back when her rare visits home were brokered by her staff, who would wait for their boss in a black-ops Winnebago out on the street. Ten years ago now? His mother was dead already, or still alive? At the time George wondered if Pattern couldn't just send a mannequin to holiday meals in her place, its pockets stuffed with money. Maybe make it edible, the face carved from lamb meat, to deepen the catharsis when they gnashed it apart with their teeth. Anyway, wouldn't his sister like to know that there was now one less person who might make a grab for her money? She could soften security at the compound, wherever she lived. Dad was dead. Probably she already knew. When you're that wealthy, changes in your biological signature, such as the sudden omission of a patriarch, show up instantly on your live update. You blink in the high-resolution mirror at your reflection, notice no change whatsoever, and then move on with your day. Maybe she'd have her personal physicians test her for sadness later in the week, just to be sure.

The question now was how to fire off an email to his very important sister that would leapfrog her spam filter, which was probably a group of human people, arms linked, blocking unwanted communications to their elusive boss, who had possibly evolved into smoke by now.

Simple was probably best. 'Dear Pat,' George wrote. 'Mom and Dad have gone out and they are not coming back. It's just you and me now. Finally we have this world to ourselves. P.S. Write back!'

George went to California to pack his father's things, intending a full-force jettison into the dumpster. He'd only just started surveying the watery one-bedroom apartment, where he could not picture his father standing, sitting, sleeping, or eating, mostly because he had trouble picturing his father at all, when a neighbor woman, worrisomely tall, came to be standing uninvited in the living room. He'd left the door open and cracked the windows so the breeze could do its work. Let the elements scrub this place free of his father. He needed candles, wind, a shaman. And on the subject of need: after sudden travel into blistering sunshine, he needed salty food to blow off in his mouth. He needed sex, if only with himself. Oh, to be alone with his laptop so he could leak a little cream onto his belly. Now there was a trespasser in his father's home, suited up in business wear. It was enormously difficult to picture such people as babies. And yet one provided the courtesy anyway. An effort to relate. Their full maturation was even harder to summon. He was apparently to believe that, over time, these creatures, just nude little seals at first, would elongate and gain words. A layer of fur would cover them, with moist parts, and teeth, and huge pockets for gathering money. Was there a website where the corporate Ichabods of the world showed off their waterworks, gave each other rubdowns, and whispered pillow talk in an invented language? Perhaps a new category beckoned.

'Oh my God. You can't be George,' the woman said.

George sort of shared her disbelief. He couldn't be. The metaphysics were troubling, if you let them get to you. But day after day, with crushing regularity, he failed to prove otherwise.

The woman approached, her nose high. Examine the specimen, she possibly thought. Maybe draw its blood.

'I can't believe it!'

He asked if he could help her. Maybe she wanted to buy something, a relic of the dead man. The realtor had said that everything had to go. Take this house down to the bones.

So far, George was just picking at the skin. He was looking through his father's takeout menus, skimming the man's Internet history. There were items of New Mexican pottery to destroy, shirts to try on.

Maybe he'd dress up like his father and take some selfies. Get the man online, if posthumously. If no one much liked him when he was alive, at least the fucker could get some likes in the afterlife. Serious.

The woman remembered herself.

'I'm Trish, Jim's . . . you know.'

'Uh-huh,' George said.

'I won't even pretend to think he might have told you about me,' Trish said. 'It's not like we were married in any real official way. At least not yet.'

Oh God. A half-wife.

The last time he spoke to his father – months ago now – George remembered not listening while his father said he had met someone, and that she – what was it? – provided the kind of service you didn't really get paid for, or paid enough, because fuck this country! And that this new girlfriend was from somewhere unique, and George knew to act impressed. Certainly his dad had seemed very proud, as if he'd met someone important from another planet.

So details had been shared, just not absorbed. Would she tell George now that his father had really loved him? Pined and whatever, wished for phone calls, had the boy's name on Google Alerts?

'Of course, Trish,' George said, and then he smacked his forehead, ever so lightly, to let her know just what he thought of his forgetfulness. She deserved as much. They embraced, at a distance, as if his father's body was stretched out between them. Then she stepped closer and really wrapped him up. He felt her breath go out of her as she collapsed against him.

George knew he was supposed to feel something. Emotional, sexual. Rage and sorrow and a little bit of predatory hunger. Even a deeper shade of indifference? History virtually demanded that the errant son, upon packing up his estranged and dead father's belongings, would seek closure with the new, younger wife. Half-wife. Some sort of circuitry demanded to be completed. He had an obligation.

It felt pretty good to hold her. She softened, but didn't go boneless. He dropped his face into her neck. Lately he'd consorted with some hug-proof men and women. They hardened when he closed in. Their bones came out. Not this one. She knew what she was doing.

'Well you sure don't smell like your father,' she said, breaking the hug. 'And you don't look like him. I mean at all.'

She laughed.

'Oh I must,' said George. He honestly didn't know.

'Nope. Trust me. I have seen that man up close. You are a very handsome young man.'

'Thank you,' said George.

'I think I want to see some ID! I might have to cry foul!'

They met later for dinner at a taco garage on the beach. Their food arrived inside what looked like an industrial metal disk.

George dug in and wished it didn't taste so ridiculously good.

'Oh my God,' he gushed.

It was sort of the problem with California, the unembarrassed way it delivered pleasure. It backed you into a corner.

After dinner they walked on the beach and tried to talk about George's father without shitting directly inside the man's urn, which was probably still ember hot. George hadn't unboxed it yet.

'I loved him, I did. I'm sure of it,' Trish said. 'When all the anger finally went out of him there was something so sweet there.'

George pictured his father deflated like a pool toy, crumpled in a corner.

'He called me by your mom's name a lot. By mistake. Rina. Irene. Boy did he do that a lot.'

'Oh, that must have been hard,' said George. Who was Irene? he wondered. Had he ever met her? His mother's name was Lydia.

'No, I get it. He had a life before me. We weren't babies. It's just that I suppose I want to be happy, too. Which is really a radical idea, if you think about it,' Trish said.

George thought about it, but he was tired and losing focus. He preferred a solitary loneliness to the kind he felt around other people. And this woman, Trish. Was she family to him now? Why did it feel like they were on a date?

'It's just that my happiness, what I needed to do to get it, threatened your father,' continued Trish.

'My father, threatened,' George said. 'But whatever could you mean?'

'Oh I like you. You're nothing like him.'

George took that in. It sounded fine, possibly true. He had no real way of knowing. He remembered his father's new radio, which he had watched him build when he was a kid, and whose dial he twisted into static for hours and hours. He could make his dad laugh by pretending the static came from his mouth, lip-syncing it. He remembered how frightened his father had been in New York when he visited. George held his arm everywhere they went. It had irritated him terribly.

What else? His father made him tomato soup once. His father slapped him while he was brushing his teeth, sending a spray of toothpaste across the mirror.

George was probably supposed to splurge on memories now. He wasn't sure he had the energy. Maybe the thing was to let the memories hurl back and cripple him, months or years from now. They needed time, wherever they were hiding, to build force, so that when they returned to smother him, he might never recover.

After their walk, they stood in a cloud of charred smoke behind the restaurant. The ocean broke and swished somewhere over a dune. Trish arched her back and yawned.

'All of this death,' she said.

'Horn-y,' George shouted. He wasn't, but still. Maybe if they stopped talking for a while they'd break this mood.

Trish tried not to laugh.

'No, uh, funny you should say that. I was just thinking, it makes me want to . . .' She smiled.

How George wished that this was the beginning of a suicide pact, after a pleasant dinner at the beach with your dead father's mistress. Just walk out together into the waves. But something told him that he knew what was coming instead.

'I'm going to comfort myself tonight, with or without you,' Trish said. 'Do you feel like scrubbing in?'

George looked away. The time was, he would sleep with anyone, of any physical style. Any make, any model. Pretty much any year. If only he could do away with the transactional phase, when the barter chips came out, when the language of seduction was suddenly spoken, rather than sung, in such non-melodious tones. It was often a deal breaker. Often. Not always.

After they'd had sex, which required one of them to leave the room to focus on the project alone, they washed up and had a drink. It felt good to sip some skank-ass, legacy whiskey from his father's Pueblo coffee mugs. Now that they'd stared into each other's cold depravity, they could relax.

Trish circled around to the inevitable.

'So what's up with Pattern?'

Here we go.

'What's she like? Are you guys in touch? Your father never would speak of her.'

Probably due to the non-disclosure agreement she must have had him sign, George figured.

'You know,' he said, pausing, as if his answer was more than ordinarily true, 'she's really nice, really kind. I think she's misunderstood.'

'Did I misunderstand it when her company, in eighteen months, caused more erosion to the Great Barrier Reef than had since been recorded in all of history?'

'She apologized for that.'

'I thought you were going to say she didn't do it. Or that it didn't happen that way.'

'No, she did do it, with great intention, I think. I bet at low tide she would have stood on the reef herself and smashed that fucking thing into crumbs for whatever fungal fuel they were mining. But, you know, she apologized. In a way, that's much better than never having done it. She has authority now. Gravity. She's human.'

'What was she before?'

Before? George thought. Before that she was his sister. She babysat for him. He once saw her get beaten up by another girl. She went to a special smart-people high school that had classes on Saturdays. Before that she was just this older person in his home. She had her own friends. She kept her door closed. Someone should have told him she was going to disappear. He would have tried to get to know her.

In the morning Trish recited the narrative she had concocted for them. Their closeness honored a legacy. Nothing was betrayed by their physical intimacy. They'd both lost someone. It was now their job to make fire in the shape of – here George lost track of her theory – George's dad.

Trish looked like she wanted to be challenged. Instead George nodded and agreed and tried to hold her. He said he thought that a fire like that would be a fine idea. Even though they'd treated each other like specimens the night before, two lab technicians straining to achieve a result, their hug was oddly platonic today. He pictured the two of them out in the snow, pouring a gasoline silhouette of his dead father. Igniting it. Effigy or burn pile?

'We didn't know each other before,' said Trish. 'Now we do. We're in each other's lives. This is real. And it's good. You're not just going to go home and forget me. It won't be possible.'

George would sign off on pretty much any press release about what had happened last night, and what they now meant to each other, so long as it featured him catching his plane at 9.30 a.m. and never seeing her again.

As he was leaving, Trish grabbed him.

'I would say "one for the road", but I don't really believe in that. Just that whole way of thinking and speaking. It sounds sorrowful and final and I don't want that to be our thing. That's not us. I don't like the word "road" and I definitely don't like the word "one". Two is much better. Two is where it's at.'

She held up two fingers and tried to get George to kiss them.

George smiled at her, pled exhaustion. It was sweet of her to offer, he said, and normally he would, but.

'You know, research shows,' Trish said, not giving up, 'that really it's a great energy boost, to love and be loved. To climax. To cause to climax. To cuddle and talk and to listen and speak. You're here! You're standing right here with me now!'

'I'm sorry,' said George. 'I guess it's all just starting to hit me. Dad. Being gone. I don't think I'd bring the right spirit right now. You would deserve better.'

It didn't feel good or right to play this card, but as he said it he found it was more true than he'd intended.

Trish was beautiful, but given the growing privacy of his sexual practice, such factors no longer seemed to matter. He would probably love to have sex with her, if she could somehow find a way of vanishing, and if the two of them could also find a way to forget that they had tried that already, last night, and the experience had been deeply medical and isolating. It was just too soon to hope for a sufficiently powerful denial to erase all that and let them, once again, look at each other like strangers, full of lust and hope.

'Is that a bad thing?' George asked his therapist, after returning home and telling her the basics.

'And please don't ask me what I think,' he continued. 'The reason people ask a question is because they would like an answer. Reflecting my question back to me, I swear, is going to make me hurl myself out of the window.'

Together they looked at the small, dirty window. There were bars on it. The office was on the ground floor.

'I'd hate to be a cause of your death,' said the therapist, unblinking.

'Well I just wonder what you think.'

'OK, but I don't think you need to lecture me in order to get me to answer a question. You seem to think I need to be educated about how to respond to you. There are also many other reasons people ask questions, aside from wanting answers. You're an imbecile if you think otherwise.'

'OK, you're right, I'm sorry.'

'Well, then, I think it must be lonely. I do. To find yourself attracted to a woman who also seems, as you say, attracted to you – if that's true – and to think you'd be more content to fantasize about her than to experience her physically. So it sounds lonely to me. But we should also notice that this is a loneliness you've chosen, based on your sexual desires. Your sexuality seems to thrive on loneliness. And I can't help but sense that some part of you is proud of that. Your story seems vaguely boastful.'

'Plus her being my father's widow.'

Dr Graco frowned.

'What was that?' she asked.

'You know, her also having been involved with my father, before he died. I guess I left that part out.'

Dr Graco took a moment to write in her notebook. She wrote quickly, and with a kind of disdain, as if she didn't like to have to make contact with the page. A fear of contaminants, maybe. A disgust with language.

It had sometimes occurred to him that therapists used this quiet writing time, after you've said something striking, or, more likely, boring, to make notes to themselves about other matters. Grocery lists, plans. One never got to see what was written down, and there was simply no possible way that all of it was strictly relevant. How much of it was sheer stalling, running out the clock? How much of it just got the narcissist in the chair across from you to shut up for a while?

She wrote through one page and had turned to another before looking up.

'I am sorry to hear about your father.'

'I should have told you. I apologize.'

'He died . . . recently?'

'Two weeks ago. That's why I was away. My missed appointment. Which I paid for, but. I was gone. I'm not sure if you . . .'

'I see. Do you mean it when you say you should have told me?'

'Well, I found the prospect of telling you exhausting, I guess. I was annoyed that I had to do it. To be honest, I wished you could just, through osmosis, have the information, in the same way you can see what I'm wearing and we don't need to discuss it. It's just a self-evident fact. You could just look at me and know that my father is dead.'

She resumed writing, but he did not want to wait for her.

'That's not a criticism of you, by the way. I don't think you were supposed to guess. I mean I don't think I think that. Maybe. You know, to just be sensitive and perceptive enough to know. I am sometimes disappointed about your powers, I guess. That's true, I should admit that. I just wish I had, like, a helper, who could run ahead of me to deliver the facts, freeing me up from supplying all of this context when I talk to people. Otherwise I'm just suddenly this guy who's like, my father died, blah blah. I'm just that guy.'

'But you weren't. Because you didn't tell me. You were not that guy.'

'Right, I guess.'

'So then who were you?'

'What?'

'You didn't want to be the guy who told me your father had died, so by not telling me, what guy did you end up being instead?'

For some reason, George saw himself and Pattern, as kids, waiting on a beach for their lunch to digest, so they could go swimming. Pattern was dutifully counting down from two thousand. It was a useless memory, irrelevant here. He remembered when he shopped and cooked for his mother, when she wasn't feeling well, and then really wasn't feeling well. He cleaned and took care of her. His father had already planted his flag in California. He was that guy, but for such a short time. Two weeks? He'd been very many people since then. Who was he when he didn't tell Dr Graco that his father died? Nobody. No one remarkable. He'd been someone too scared or too bored, he didn't know which, to discuss something important.

'That just made me think of something,' he said finally. 'The word "guy". I don't know. Have you heard of Guy Fox?'

'I assume you don't mean the historic figure, Guy Fawkes?'

'No. F-o-x. Porn star, but that's not really a good label for what he does. It's not clear you can even call it porn anymore. It's so sort of remote and kind of random, and definitely not obviously sexual. Or even at all. I mean almost, just, boredom. Anyway, it's a new sort of thing. He provides eye contact. People pay a lot. He'll just watch you, on video. You can stream him to your TV, and he'll watch you. People pay him to watch while they have sex, of course, or masturbate, but now supposedly people just hire him to watch them while they hang out alone in their houses. Whenever they look up, he's looking at them. They are paying to have eye contact whenever they want. They want someone out there seeing them. And he's just amazing. Apparently there's nothing quite like getting seen by him. It's an addiction.'

'Ah, I see. Well I'm afraid we have to stop.'

Afraid, afraid, afraid. Don't be afraid, George thought. Embrace it.

For once he wished she'd say, 'I'm delighted our session is over, George, now get the fuck out of my office, you monster.'

Bowing to a certain protocol of the bereaved, George acquired a baby dog: hairless, pink and frightening. His therapist had put him onto it after he kept insisting he was fine. She explained that people who lose a parent, especially one they weren't close to, tend to grieve their lack of grief. Like they want to really feel something, and don't, and so they grieve that. That absence. She said that one solution to this circular, masturbatory grief, is to take care of something. To be responsible for another living creature.

Except George and the animal had turned out to be a poor match. That's how he put it to the dogcatcher, or whatever the man was called when he sent the wet thing back, and then hired cleaners to sanitize his home. The animal was more like a quiet young child, waiting for a ride, determined not to exploit any hospitality whatsoever in George's home. It rarely sprawled out, never seemed to relax. It sat upright in the corner, sometimes trotting to the window, where it glanced up and down the street, patiently confirming that it had been abandoned. Would it recognize rescue when it came? Sometimes you just had to wait this life out, it seemed to be thinking, and get a better deal next time. God knows where the fucking thing slept. Or if.

Did the animal not get tired? Did it not require something? George would occasionally hose off the curry from the unmolested meat in his takeout container, and scrape it into the dog bowl, only to clean it up, untouched, days later. The animal viewed these meals with calm detachment. How alienating it was, to live with a creature so ungoverned by appetites. This thing could go hungry. It had a long game. What kind of level playing field was that? George felt entirely outmatched.

One night George tried to force the issue. He wanted more from it, and it wanted absolutely nothing from George, so perhaps, as the superior species, with broader perspective in the field, George needed to step up and trigger change. Be a leader. Rule by example. Maybe he had been playing things too passive? He pulled the thing onto his lap. He stroked its wet, stubbled skin, put on one of those TV shows that pets are supposed to like. No guns, just soft people swallowing each other.

The dog survived the affection. It trembled under George's hands. Some love is strictly clinical. Maybe this was like one of those deep-tissue massages that releases difficult feelings? George forced his hand along the dog's awful back, wondering why anyone would willingly touch another living thing. What a disaster of feelings it stirred up, feelings that seemed to have no purpose other than to suffocate him. Finally the dog turned in George's lap, as if standing on ice, and carefully licked its master's face. Just once, and briefly. A studied, scientific lick, using the tongue to gain important information. Then it bounced down to its corner again, where it sat and waited.

M onths after his father's death there was still no word from Pattern. After he'd returned from California, and cleansed himself in the flat, gray atmosphere of New York, George had sent her another email, along the lines of, 'Hey Pat, I'm back. I've got Dad's dust. Let me know if you want to come say goodbye to it. There are still some slots free. Visiting hours are whenever you fucking want. —G.'

He never heard back, and figured he wasn't going to – on the Internet now Pattern was referred to as a fugitive wanted by Europol, for crimes against the environment – but one night, getting into bed, his phone made an odd sound. Not its typical ring. It took him a minute to track the noise to his phone, and at first he thought it must be broken, making some death noise before it finally shut down.

He picked it up and heard a long, administrative pause.

'Please hold for Pattern,' a voice said.

He waited and listened. Finally a woman said hello.

'Hello?' said George. 'Pattern?'

'Who's this?' It wasn't Pattern. This person sounded like a bitchy tween, entitled and shrill.

'You called me,' explained George.

'Who's on the line,' said the teenager, 'or I'm hanging up.'

George was baffled. Did a conversation with his sister really require such a cloak-and-dagger ground game? He hung up the phone.

The phone rang again an hour later, and it was Pattern herself.

'Jesus, George, what the fuck? You hung up on my staff?'

'First of all, Hello,' he said. 'Secondly, let's take a look at the transcript and I'll show you exactly what happened. Your team could use some human behavior training. But forget all that. What on earth is new, big sister?'

She wanted to see him, she said, and she'd found a way for that to be possible. They had things to discuss.

'No shit,' said George. He couldn't believe he was actually talking to her.

'Wait so where are you?' she asked. 'I don't have my thing with me.'

'What thing.'

'I mean I don't know where you are.'

'And your thing would have told you? Have you been tracking me?'

'Oh c'mon, you asshole.'

'I'm in New York.'

She laughed.

'What?'

'No, it's just funny. I mean it's funny that you still call it that.'

'What would I call it?'

'No, nothing, forget it. I'm sorry. I'm just on a different, it's, I'm thinking of something else. Forget it.'

'O-kay. You are so fucking weird and awkward. I'm not really sure I even want to see you.'

'Georgie!'

'Kidding, you freak. Can you like send a jet for me? Or a pod? Or what the fuck is it you guys even make now? Can you break my face into dust and make it reappear somewhere?'

'Ha ha. I'll send a car for you. Tomorrow night. Seven o'clock.'

George met Pattern in the sky bar of a strange building, which somehow you could not see from the street. Everyone had thought the developers had purchased the air rights and then very tastefully decided not to use them. Strike a blow for restraint. The elevator said otherwise. This thing was a fucking tower. How had they done that? The optics for that sort of thing, Pattern explained to him, had been around for fifteen years or more. Brutally old-fashioned technology. Practically caveman. She thought it looked cheesy at this point.

'A stealth scraper,' said George, wanting to sound appreciative.

'Hardly. It's literally smoke and mirrors,' Pattern said. 'I am not fucking kidding. And it's kind of gross. But whatever. I love this bar. These cocktails are fucking violent. There's a frozen pane of pork in this one. Ridiculously thin. They call it pork glass.'

'Yum,' said George, absently.

The funny thing about the bar, which was only just dawning on George, was that it was entirely free of people. And deadly silent. Out the window was a view of the city he'd never seen. Whenever he looked up he had the sensation that he was somewhere else. In Europe. In the past. On a film set. Asleep. Every now and then a young woman crept out from behind a curtain to touch Pattern on the wrist, moving her finger back and forth. Pattern would smell her wrist, make a face, and say something unintelligible.

But here she was, his very own sister. It was like looking at his mother and his father and himself, but refined, the damaged cells burned off. The best parts of them, contained in this one person.

'First of all, George,' Pattern said. 'Dad's girlfriend? Really?'

'Trish?'

'What a total pig you are. Does this woman need to be abused and neglected by two generations of our family?'

'How could you know anything about that?'

'Oh cut it out. It astonishes me when I meet people who still think they have secrets. It's so quaint! You understand that even with your doors closed and lights out . . . Please tell me you understand. I couldn't bear it if you were that naive. My own brother.'

'I understand, I think.'

'That man you pay to watch you while you're cleaning the house? On your laptop screen?'

'Guy Fox.'

'Oh, George, you are a funny young man.'

'That's actually a fairly mainstream habit, to have a watcher.'

'Right, George, it's happening all over the Middle East, too. A worldwide craze. In Poland they do it live. It's called a peeping Tom. But who cares. Baby brother is a very strange bird.

'So,' she said, scooting closer to him and giving him a luxurious hug. 'Mom and Dad never told you, huh?'

'Told me what?'

'They really never told you?'

'I'm listening.'

'I'm just not sure it's for me to say. Mom and Dad talked about it kind of a lot, I mean we all did. I just figured they'd told you.'

'What already, Jesus. There's no one else left to tell me.'

'You were adopted. That's actually not the right word. Dad got in trouble at work and his boss forced him to take you home and raise you. You were born out of a donkey's ass. Am I remembering correctly? That doesn't sound right. From the ass of an ass.'

He tried to smile.

'I'm just kidding, George, Jesus. What is wrong with people?'

'Oh my God, right?' said George. 'Why can't people entertain more stupid jokes at their own expense? Je-sus. It's so frustrating! When, like, my world view isn't supported by all the little people beneath me? And I can't demean people and get an easy laugh? It's so not fair!'

'Oh fuck off, George.'

They smiled. It felt really good. This was just tremendously nice.

'You don't understand,' he said, trying harder than usual to be serious. 'Mom punted so long ago I can't even remember her smell. And Dad was just a stranger, you know? He was so formal, so polite. I always felt like I was meeting him for the first time.'

He tried to sound like his father, like any father: 'Hello, George, how are you? How was your flight? Well that's grand. What's your life like these days?'

Pattern stared at him.

'Honestly,' said George. 'I can't stand making small talk with people who have seen me naked. Or who fed me. Or spanked me. I mean once you spank someone, you owe them a nickname. Was that just me or were Mom and Dad like completely opposed to nicknames? Or even just Honey or Sweetie or any of that.'

'Jesus, George, what do you want from people? You have some kind of intimacy fantasy. Do you think other people go around hugging each other and holding hands, mainlining secrets and confessions into each other's veins?'

'I have accepted the fact of strangers,' said George. 'After some struggle. But it's harder when they are in your own family.'

'Violin music for you,' said Pattern, and she snapped her fingers.

He looked up, perked his ears, expecting to hear music.

'Wow,' she marveled. 'You think I'm very powerful, don't you?'

'Honestly, I don't know. I have no idea. Are you in trouble? Everything I read is so scary.'

'I am in a little bit of trouble, yes. But don't worry. It's nothing. And you. You seem so sad to me,' Pattern said. 'Such a sad, sad young man.' She stroked his face, and it felt ridiculously, treacherously comforting.

George waved this off, insisted that he wasn't. He just wanted to know about her. He really did. Who knows where she'd vanish to after this, and he genuinely wanted to know what her life was like, where she lived. Was she married? Had she gotten married in secret or something?

'I don't get to act interested and really mean it,' George explained. 'I mean ever, so please tell me who you are. It's kind of a selfish question, because I can't figure some things out about myself, so maybe if I hear about you, something will click.'

'Me? I tend to date the house-husband type. Self-effacing, generous, asexual. Which is something I'm really attracted to, I should say. Men with Low T, who go to bed in a full rack of pajamas. That's my thing. I don't go for the super-carnal hetero men; they seem like zoo animals. Those guys who know what they want, and have weird and highly developed skills as lovers, invariably have the worst possible taste – we're supposed to congratulate them for knowing that they like to lick butter right off the stick. What a nightmare, to be subject to someone else's expertise. The guys I tend to date, at first, are out to prove that they endorse equality, that my career matters, that my interests are primary – they make really extravagant displays of selflessness, burying all of their own needs. I go along with it, and over time I watch them deflate and lose all reason to live, by which point I have steadily lost all of my attraction for them. I imagine something like that is mirrored in the animal kingdom, but honestly that's not my specialty. I should have an airgun in my home so I could put these guys out of their misery. Or a time-lapse video documenting the slow and steady loss of self-respect they go through. It's a turn-off, but, you know, it's my turn-off. Part of what initially arouses me is the feeling that I am about to mate with someone who will soon be ineffectual and powerless. I've come to rely on the arc. It's part of my process.'

'You think these guys don't mean it that they believe in equality?'

'No, I think they do, and that it has a kind of cost. They just distort themselves so much trying to do the right thing that there's nothing left.'

'And you enjoy that?'

'Well, they enjoy that. They're driven to it. I'm just a bystander to their quest. And I enjoy that. It's old school, but I like to watch.'

'So you are basically fun times to date.'

'I pull my weight, romantically. I'm not stingy. I supply locations.

I supply funding. Transportation. I'm kind of an executive producer. I can green-light stuff.'

'Nobody cums unless you say so, right?'

'That's not real power,' she said, as if such a thing was actually under her control. She frowned. 'That's bookkeeping. Not my thing at all. Anyway, I think the romantic phase of my life is probably over now. My options won't be the same. Freedom.'

'Jail time?' asked George.

'It's not exactly jail for someone like me. But it's fine if you imagine it that way. That would be nice.'

George hated to do it. They were having such a good time, and she must get this a lot, but he was her last living blood relative and didn't he merit some consideration over all the hangers-on who no doubt lived pretty well by buzzing around in her orbit?

'All right, so, I mean, you're rich, right? Like insanely so?'

Pattern nodded carefully.

'You could, like, buy anything?'

'My money is tied up in money,' Pattern said. 'It's hard to explain. You get to a point where a big sadness and fatigue takes over.'

'Not me,' said George. 'I don't. Anyway, I mean, it wouldn't even make a dent for you to, you know, solve my life financially. Just fucking solve it. Right?'

Pattern smiled at him, a little too gently, he thought. It seemed like a bad-news smile.

'You know the studies, right?'

Dear God Jesus. 'What studies?'

'About what happens when people are given a lot of money. People like you, with the brain and appetites of an eleven-year-old.'

'Tell me.' He'd let the rest of the comment go.

'It's not good.'

'Well I don't fucking want it to be good. I want it to be fun.'

'I don't think it's very fun, either, I'm afraid.'

'Don't be afraid, Pattern. Leave that to me. I will be very afraid,

I will be afraid for two, and never have to worry about money again. Depraved, sordid, painful. I'll go for those. Let me worry about how it will feel.'

Pattern laughed into her drink.

'Sweet, sweet Georgie,' she said.

I t was getting late, and the whispering interruptions had increased, Pattern's harried staff scurrying around them, no doubt plotting the extraction. An older gentleman in a tuxedo came out to their couch and held up a piece of paper for Pattern, at eye level, which, to George, sitting right next to her, looked perfectly blank.

Pattern studied it, squinting, and sighed. She shifted in her seat.

'Armageddon,' said George. 'Time to wash my drones with my drone towel!'

Pattern didn't smile.

'I hate to say it, little George, but I think I'm going to have to break this up.'

He didn't like this world, standing up, having to leave. Everything had seemed fine back on the couch.

'Here,' Pattern said, giving him a card. 'Send your bills to William.'

'Ha ha.'

'What?'

'Your joke. That you obviously don't even know you just made.'

She was checking her phone, not listening.

On the street they hugged for a little while and tried to say good-bye. A blue light glowed from the back seat of Pattern's car. George had no idea who she was, what she really did, or when he would ever see her again.

'Do you think I can be in your life,' George asked. 'I'm not sure why but it feels scary to ask you that.'

He tried to laugh.

'Oh, you are, George,' said Pattern. 'Here you are. In my life right now. Closer to me than anyone else on the planet.'

'You know what I mean. How can I reach you?' He didn't

particularly want to say goodbye to her.

'I always know where you are, Georgie. I do. Trust me.'

'But I don't know that. I don't really feel that. It doesn't feel like you're even out there. When you're not here it's like you never were here at all.'

'No, no,' she whispered. 'I don't believe that. That's not true.'

'Is something going to happen to you? I don't know what to believe.'

'Well,' she said. 'Something already has. Something has happened to all of us, right?'

'Please don't make a joke or be clever, Elizabeth. I can't stand it. There's nobody left but you. What if I don't see you again? What will I do?'

'Oh Georgie, I am right here. I am right here with you now.'

George kept quiet about his sister in therapy. He talked about everything else. But sometimes he'd catch Dr Graco studying him, and he'd think that perhaps she knew. She didn't need to be told. She might not grasp the specific details, the bare facts – who and when and what and all those things that did not matter – but it seemed to George that she could see, or was starting to, that someone out there was seeing him, watching him. That someone really knew him and that, whatever else you could say about him, it was clear that he was no longer really alone.

At home George listened, and hoped, and waited, but his phone never made the strange tone again. He found nothing on his sister in the news, though he looked. Whoever had been calling for her blood had gone quiet. And George couldn't decide if their silence meant that they'd lost interest, or that they had her, they got her, and Pattern was gone.

One night it was late and he'd let his uncertainty overpower him. It had been a year since he'd seen her. Where was she? How could she just disappear? He'd been saving up his idea for a moment just like this one, so he sat down at his desk and wrote his sister an email.

Elizabeth—

Is it just me now, or are you still out there? Don't write back. I cannot imagine how busy you must be! There is a lot that I cannot imagine. But that's OK, right? You're out there looking, I know. I am waving at you, wherever you are. I am down here saying hello. I love you very much.

Your brother,

George ■

© BRYANT AUSTIN
A Mother Listens, 2006

WHALE FALL

Rebecca Giggs

A few years ago I helped push a beached humpback whale back
out into the sea, only to witness it return and expire under its
own weight on the sand. For the three days that it died the whale
was a public attraction. People brought their children down to see it.
They would stand in the surf and wave babies in pastel rompers over
the whale, as if to catch the drift of an evaporating myth. The whale
was black like piano wood and because it was still young, it was pink
in the joints under its fins. Every few minutes it exhaled loudly and
slammed its fluke against the sand – a tantrum or leverage. Its soft
chest turned slack, concertinaed, when it rolled.

At first the mood was festive. People cheered every time the whale
wrestled in the breakers. Efforts made to free it from a sandbar in the
morning had been aided by the tide. That the whale had re-stranded,
this time higher up the beach, did not portend well for its survival but
so astonished were the crowd and such a marvel was the animal that
immoderate hope proved difficult to quash. What the whale inspired
was wonderment, a dilation of the ordinary. Everyone was talking
about it, on the buses and in the delis. There were dogs on the beach
held back by their owners, sweeping flat quarter-circles in the sand
with their tails. How they imagined the whale – predator, prey or
distant relation – was anyone's guess, but the dogs seemed keen to

get a closer look. At sunset armfuls of grease-blotted butchers' paper, chips and battered hake were passed around. The local lifesavers distributed zip-up hoodies. Wildlife officers, who had been standoffish with the gathering crowd, relaxed and taught some lessons on whale physiology.

'Whales are mammals,' they began, 'as we are too.' This surprised those who were accustomed to thinking of all marine animals as species of fish. They raised their eyebrows and nodded along. Cetacean – from the ancient Greek *kētos*, made Latinate as *cetus*: an order of mammals that includes whales, dolphins and porpoises. 'Under its skin the whale is wrapped in a subcutaneous envelope of fat called blubber.' Trying to imagine the properties of blubber I could only conjure those agar desserts sold in Asian supermarkets: opaque, calorie-rich and more rigid than their wobble suggests. While in the ocean its blubber fat insulates the whale and allows the animal to maintain a constant inner temperature. Out of the ocean, the blubber smothers it.

'That whale has the opposite problem to hypothermia,' the wildlife officers explained. Though we were now shivering, the whale – only metres away – was boiling alive in the kettle of itself.

A group of us slept lightly in the dunes, arrayed like question marks and commas on the white sand. Our minds cast to the cetacean huffing beyond the swale, then swooped into softer visions. I woke to the sounds of surfers arriving in the dark. Were those sharks raiding a lux channel tipped up by the moon? Hard to tell. We resolved that the whale had been washed too high on the beach for any shark to reach it. Every detail, peculiar and particular, rinsed by pewter light. Ridges in the sand. Plants like handfuls of knives. It felt cold to us.

In the morning a part of the whale that ought not to be outside of it was outside of it. A digestive organ, frilled and pale in the foam. The whale's billiard-ball eyes tumbled in its head and its breathing sounded laboured. The sharks slid into vapour, a squinting rumour. No blood on the tideline. People stayed back from the water nonetheless. Swept slantwise, shallow waves smoothed, over-smoothed, smoothed. I palmed an ordinary shell which still sits on my window ledge. A cordon was set up. Seagulls flew down to peck avian hieroglyphs in the whale's back. At every nip it flinched, still intensely alive and tormented.

Walking off some agitation I'd accrued watching the birds, I found one of the wildlife officers crouched a way down the beach. A blocky guy wearing wrap-around sunglasses, his jaw was set tight. The whale's central nervous system was so large and complex, he explained, that euthanising it in the manner that one might kill a cow or an old horse was impossible. A bolt through the brain would take too long for the heart to register it; a shock to the heart wouldn't transmit to the brain instant death. Suffering was inevitable and visible.

There came a point when strapping the whale with dynamite was the most humane option, but the clean-up afterwards – particularly when the whale had run aground on a popular public beach – was expensive. (How expensive? In time I'd look it up. Another whale, found dead nearby a few seasons hence, cost AUS$188,000 to remove. The council and the State Fisheries Department disputed who should foot the bill. 'Because it's a mammal, not a fish, they believe it's not in their jurisdiction,' said the mayor.)

The wildlife officer and I stared to the horizon. The sea mouthed our shoes. Then we walked up to his van so he could show me the shot.

'It's called the Green Dream,' he said.

The needle was at least a foot long and as thick as a car aerial. A rubber tube ran to a pump container. The whole apparatus was reminiscent of something you might use to administer herbicide in the garden; so much so that the sight of it brought on a blast of greenhouse smells (mint-ammonia-smoke, trapped heat). The liquid was a fluorescent, acid green. It might work, he speculated, because the whale was only a yearling. But you wouldn't want to get the dosage wrong. Whose was the dream, I wondered? The officer let me hold it for a minute, this ghastly prop, heavier than it looked. I pictured the whale's many netted veins and arteries which, if you could unpick them, would extend a hundred metres down the beach like the delicate red thread from a smashed thermometer.

Later I asked, 'Is it you who makes the decision?' I knew he could get a legal gun instead, and use it. He held his hand crab-like on the wet sand and said nothing.

People were still eating from lunch boxes, taking phone calls and posing for photographs in front of the whale. Then someone came down from the dunes with a wreath of plaited seagrasses and pigface flowers and proposed laying it over the whale's forehead. The surfers took a knee in prayer or shame, their wetsuits half peeled to expose tattoos of constellations and regional creeds. A toddler started to cry and the whale made a cracked, tubular noise. Everyone tightened in the chest and ribs. A few families turned away. Stillness stepped through the crowd: desperation; vigil.

I asked the wildlife officer what would happen afterwards and he told me that they'd arranged for two mechanical bobcats to come and collect the carcass. 'Beach and bundle,' he called it, the policy. The whale would be chainsawed in half and transported to the Tamala Park tip in Mindarie to decay amid the household waste and disused white goods. After death its putrefaction would generate yet more heat, scorching its bones and burning its organs black: if they didn't cut it up, it would explode. Was the council concerned a dead whale would attract malingering hammerheads and thresher sharks were they to tow it back out? I was confused about why the animal was destined for the junkyard.

'This whale is malnourished,' he offered. 'We don't know why. Maybe he's sick, maybe the mother didn't feed it right as a calf. Maybe the whale's consumed plastic or it's poisoned somehow, with parasites, or too tired to eat. Looks like it's been attacked before it beached.' He cleaned salt spots off his sunglasses. I saw his eyes were tired. 'Killer whales pick off the weak ones,' he said.

A swathe of silence passed between us, gulls like asterisks overhead. 'There's an argument, a conservation argument, not to put a whale that's been weeded out back in again.'

That year forty-six whales ran aground along the Western Australian coastline. The year before there had been just thirteen, and in the years that followed the number returned to the mid-teens. Spectators on the beach that day had their suspicions. A comet had flared icily over Rottnest Island the previous week. The much-adored Antarctic Blue whale skeleton in the Western Australian Museum in Perth was set to be lifted out of the roof on a crane and dismantled. (At long last, would it be returned to the sea?) Someone's sister talked of significant and recent naval operations. And wasn't the weather undeniably weird all the time now? An El Niño year. Bitter mention was made by many of 'The Japanese'; of the trauma and exhaustion of whales chased by harpoons. Almost certainly, it was said by one man, the Nyungar elders predicted the humpback – that's why they weren't there. What was happening was sour, something dark. A bad business for the land.

I distrusted the inflection in their voices even as I too brimmed with guesswork, troubled by the whale from afar. Offered in candour these theories were conspiratorial; premised on the assumption of unspoken consensus struck on the existence of deeper streams of logic running behind the frail authority of science, biology and the wildlife officers' superintendence of the whale. Narratives in those tones could prove no whale-beaching hypothesis to the crowd's satisfaction. Their loyalty was to the unverifiable hunch, to intuited patterns of allegory, augury or plot. As if the whale itself, in its fleshly presence, testified to hitherto unfathomed dimensions of reality. Or so it seemed then, as the sun found its zenith and the temperature climbed.

One woman broke free from the crowd and strode into the water with the wreath in her fists overhead. She sang clearly. It took three wildlife officers to pull her off the side of the whale, kicking. She had spiritual reasons, she said. She had spiritual *skills*. Her fury wasn't dignified. It was incandescent. But the whale never wore the sodden wreath.

When I searched later for reasons why humpbacks founder, I learned that in the coastal currents some whales become entangled in abandoned fishing kit or ingest trash – bags, wrappers and mesh. Because they are so well insulated by that thick layer of blubber they attract fat-soluble toxins as well, absorbing heavy metals and inorganic compounds found in pesticides, fertilizers and the other pollutants that powder the modern sea. The body of a whale is a magnifier for these insidious agrochemicals because cetaceans live a long time and accrue a toxic load from their prey. Levels build up over many seasons, making some animals far more polluted than their surrounding environment.

I read that estuarine beluga in Canada had been found to be so noxious that their carcasses were classified as toxic waste for disposal. Tissue sampling of sperm whales around the world revealed quantities of cadmium that would kill living cells in a lab. (Cadmium, a compound found in paint and industrial manufacturing, and a by-product of burning fossil fuels, causes metal fume fever, fluid in the lungs, kidney disease and cancer in humans.) The most polluted animals on the face of the earth were thought to be American killer whales in Puget Sound, a place where the starfish had been observed actually melting. The data supported a highly improbable hypothesis, even given the levels of contaminants in the area: that the whales had been chewing batteries or drinking flame retardant to supplement their marine dinners.

I thought of the humpback in the dump. The whale as landfill. It was a metaphor, and then it wasn't.

Swirled through blubber, scientists believed these stored chemicals remained 'metabolically inert', which is to say they didn't harm otherwise healthy whales because they weren't metabolized and recirculated through the animal's organs. The effects on humans who ate whales, however, were reportedly much more pernicious.

I read that Greenland's Inuit women, who seasonally consume whale meat, whale skin and fat as part of a traditional diet, had been warned off beluga during pregnancy and advised to stop breastfeeding their babies altogether. These women may occupy some of the most isolated and deindustrialized regions in the world, but sustaining themselves on whales had made their bodies into sites of concentrated contamination. Nearly all the Inuit people who had been tested had levels of mercury and organochlorides that exceeded World Health Organization Standards. When a whale begins to starve, as when it is stranded, its body reverts to ketosis – breaking down blubber for energy in the absence of food. Stored toxins then cease to be dormant and are released back into the bloodstream. This can poison the whale from within, just as it harms those people who eat blighted whale meat. The humpbacks that stream along the Australian coast on their annual migrations are less likely to be afflicted with a chemical ballast as cetacean species elsewhere – these animals spend much of their life cycle in the comparatively benign Southern Ocean (though these waters are also now changing). But the fact that whales were turning up in many other places around the globe full of industrial by-products, plastic and pesticide seemed to me to cast gloom over the intangible symbolism of whales everywhere, and here.

In the weeks that followed the beaching I found myself preoccupied with an unhappy idea. Our feelings about the dying whale, what it signified and how to save it, might have been misplaced. Chiefly what we talked about, when we talked about whales, was how we'd learned to leave them in the sea, to stop taking them from the wild. This was a self-satisfied story to tell in Australia, a story that was as much about our human capacity for benevolence and awe as it was about the resilience of other species. But what if we were now taking the wildness out of the whale? If deep inside whales the indelible imprint of humans could be found, could we go on recounting the myth of their remarkable otherness, their strange, wondrous and vast animalian world? It struck me that the green dream, lethal and serene, might have been ours after all.

REBECCA GIGGS

H ere is a story I heard on the beach, about whales that die very
far out to sea, perhaps of old age or ship strike. If they are
not washed into shallower water by the wind and tides, their massive
bodies eventually sink, and simultaneously decay as they sink; they
are continuously pecked at by fish, swimming crabs, amphipods
and sharks attracted to the carcass. It takes a long time. Weeks,
months. Later the whale will slip below the depth where epipelagic
foragers can feed off it. As the pressure compounds, the whale's body
decelerates in its fall, and putrefying gases build up in its softening
tissues. It drifts past fish that no longer look like anything we might
call fish, but bottled fireworks, reticulated rigging and musical
instruments turned inside out. The whale enters the abyssopelagic
zone. No light has ever shone here, for so long as the world has had
water. Purblind hagfish creep, jawless, pale as the liberated internal
organs of other sea animals. The only sound is the tickly scrunch of
brittle stars, splitting themselves in half and eating one another alive.
Slowly. It is very cold. Hell's analogue on earth. Hagfish rise to meet
the carcass and tunnel in, lathering their burrows with mucus. They
absorb whalish nutrients through their skin.

The whale body reaches a point where the buoyancy of its meat
and organs is only tethered down by the force of its falling bones.
Methane is released in minuscule bubbles. It scatters skin and
sodden flesh below it, upon which grows a carpet of white worms
waving upwards (grass on its grave). Then, sometimes, the entire
whale skeleton will suddenly burst through the cloud of its carcass.
For a time, the skeleton might stay hitched jerkily at the spine to its
parachute of muscle; a macabre marionette dangling in the slight
currents. Then it drops, falls quickly to the sea floor, into the plush
cemetery of the worms. Gusts of billowing silt roll away. The mantle
of the whale's pulpier parts settles over it. Marine snow (anonymous
matter, ground to a salt in the lighter layers of the sea) beats down
ceaselessly. Rat-tails, devouring snails and more polychaetes appear.
The bones are stripped and then fluff up with silver-white bacteria,
so that it appears as if the skeleton is draped in metres of downy

towelling. Years may pass, decades even, before there is nothing left except a dent that holds the dark darker.

Whales are conscious breathers, which means they have to remember to do it. Towards the end, low tide and a small group persisting, I shuffled in close to hear its irregular gasps. The whale's eye – midnight, mid-ocean – had no eyelashes and, according to another wildlife officer, no tear ducts (for what would be the point of crying in the sea?). I hovered as near as I was able to, speaking sometimes to the whale's blowhole. What felt important in that moment was the act of seeing this through to the end, of agreeing not to leave the whale alone. Kinship, I guess, was what we proffered. Who could say if it was more or less welcome than the barbiturate injection still packed up in the van? No one clicked a cartridge into a rifle or brandished the merciful stick of explosive. Nature, as they say, would run its course. That was a phrase we trusted. We repeated it.

Inside the whale it grew hotter and hotter, though that proved difficult to imagine. We humans, I think, devise death as a gradual loss of fire; the gleam retracted from every corner, pulled to a wick within, guttering out. The whale's descent was different. I had an idea of each sentence as I spoke it, cool and round as a stone, dropping for five minutes or longer down into the whale's head. But what did the whale understand by my speech? A germane sound, inlaid with information, or just noise, background babble as the wind speaks in the trees, as dogs bark, being dragged off by their owners on leashes. Do human voices sound as ethereal to the whale as whale voices sound to us? Or do we scratch and irritate the whale, a pin in the ear?

I put one hand briefly on the skin of the whale and felt its distant heartbeat, an electrical throbbing like a refrigerator. Life on that scale – *mammalian* life on that scale – so unfamiliar and familiar simultaneously. Oh, the alien whale. The world-bound whale. A net of shadows spread out across the ribby sand. All of us swayed slightly on the spot. By-catch. The occasional plosive rush of air, less frequent. The mumbling of the tide in the tiny bays of the sea. ■

LADY NEPTUNE

Ann Beattie

M rs Edward R. was pushed into the building in a wheelchair with a half-sized seat, several straps pulled not exactly tightly, but tightly enough, over her lap. She loved, loved those skirts from several years ago, weighted at the bottom and voluminous, with ruched sides billowing below the stitches into parachutes – so comfortable, so (as is said) forgiving.

But of course, with a real parachute you'd be up in the air, dangling above the Atlantic. Blowing right past the condos overlooking the water, such as 1800 Atlantic, where her son Darryl lived with the nicer of his twin sons following an abominable stroke when he was fifty-six: a non-smoker; a jogger; okay – a few too many recreational drugs in his youth. Darryl spent many days on the balcony, staring at the water. She didn't do that – she wasn't in that sort of shape, thank God – but she did sometimes cross her eyes and look at nothing as a way of introspecting.

She was being carried into the building's private elevator, key-activated so that everyone else coming to the party would have to climb the stairs, regardless of age, infirmity, fame. That, or they'd already know better than to come. Only for her, only for Alva, did the host admit to having the key. 'Alvie,' he'd said to her years ago, 'it's our little secret.' Among their other little secrets was that they sent the cook away and had a flute of champagne with lunch, and that they'd found an accountant who had ingenious ways for his clients to cheat on their taxes. Her husband R. (that was their nasty nickname for him. He'd read too many Russian novels.) had never particularly liked Duncan Oswald, though he, too, had usually gone to Duncan's annual Christmas party. It was a small community, and one didn't want to give offense by not attending. Still, one year R. had sent Alva along without him – back when she simply walked places – and sent flowers the next day with a note of apology about his ostensible last-minute nausea, but the florist had gotten the orders mixed up, so Duncan – who always did like R., or at least appreciate that he was often wittingly or not the occasion for fun – received a bouquet of tulips with a dirty note about how their dowsing heads wanted to be you-know-where. It was Key West, so of course the florist had just written down whatever message the caller gave. Though he had nothing to do with the mix-up, obviously, R. resented Duncan for the amount of kidding he'd had to endure: Duncan had spread this story around, he hadn't.

Ned, the less-nice of her grandsons, was accompanying her. At this very moment, he was squeezing into the little elevator, placing a hand on her shoulder. The elevator's slowness made him nervous. 'Here we go,' he said tensely. He had nothing else to say as they ascended. She plucked up a bit of fabric so that it fell even lower on her leg – she hoped low enough to obscure the bruise. She couldn't get into pantyhose anymore, and she detested those stockings that ended just at the knee. That scam was always somehow humiliatingly revealed, and then you felt worse, and the person seeing felt worse.

Less-Nice Ned (she and Duncan had agreed on this, over a little Taittinger) was on best behavior tonight, for whatever reason. Duncan's cook (who had previously been a burglar in Miami; he got early parole because it was a first offense, and the prison was filled to bursting) almost collided with her grandson as the elevator door opened, in his haste to be helpful. Less-Nice Ned rolled her forward as the cook swept away imaginary obstacles, including a full-body block of a potted hibiscus at least eight feet away from the wheelchair.

Christmas lights twinkled around the pot. They twinkled from the ceiling beams, hanging like little glittering stalactites. Soon Gay Santa would appear, to change into his faux-edgy costume and perform the annual ritual of handing out small wrapped presents to all the people. You could really end up on the short end of the stick, sometimes. The previous year, one guest had received a package of airplane peanuts.

Her present, though, was a promissory note: 'My devotion forever, and my cook for your birthday, who will prepare dinner for up to ten friends.' Very generous! And yes – she had ten friends. Especially if you counted her son and his two boys, though her son would not attend, even if he said he would, and probably if Less-Nice Ned got a better offer, he'd cancel at the last minute. Her accountant and his wife would be there. Her psychiatrist. Jeannelle, who walked her dog every night (somebody not worth inviting walked the dog in the morning and mid-afternoon). Marie and Harry would be there. Maybe the Perrys. The cook, himself. Shouldn't she include the cook, and of course the gift-giver? Was that ten, or more than ten?

She settled on the sofa this way: the narrow wheelchair was turned sideways, with the cook fanning dust out of the air, as if its settling might somehow interfere with the transfer. (There was no dust; the cook also cleaned.) Next, she slid one-two-three (moving prematurely on 'two'), with her grandson's hand lightly curled under her armpit, guiding her along what even she could see was a short, sideways bump on to the Naugahyde sectional sofa. Under the cushion, she knew, were books. Duncan put them there because otherwise the cushion sank down too much, and rising would be difficult. Three decorative pillows in varying shades of green were available to be placed behind her back, if she might want to sit a little farther forward. She wasn't sure about that; it made a person look too eager, too truly on the edge of the chair.

Ah! It was very comfortable, but books or not, she was not pleased about the amount of armpit pressure that would have to be applied at the end of the evening. Still, she looked up and gave a small smile and nodded. 'Everything comfortable?' the cook said. He always spoke with bravado. He had found God while in jail, but had given Him up the second he was paroled. Also, he knew they drank champagne – she'd seen him peeking once, before he left – but what did he care? What might the cook truly care about? He was not a person she would have known in her youth. Old people couldn't meet anyone new – other people looked right through you. And her friends; she didn't want to know any more about them.

'If you could have anything in the world, what might that be?' she said to the cook.

He looked momentarily confused, as if someone might be standing behind his back. 'A lot of money,' he said.

She considered this. It seemed an honest answer. Also, just because she was old and in not very good shape, why should she be allowed a follow-up question? So she didn't ask it. It would be taking advantage of his position. Making a monkey of him. You could only talk about a zebra's stripes because they didn't speak. Now, it was turning out that if you said something about a monkey, the monkey would probably understand entirely and even consider an ironic reply. Or was that gorillas? What was Koko?

'My husband was a great believer in mutual funds. In diversifying. But I do understand that you have to have money in order to "grow your money". Even grass doesn't grow on its own. Or at least you have to water it and not let anyone walk on it and then worry about it for the rest of your life, those times it does take.'

'Ma'am,' he said.

'Well, that's enough of *that* conversation,' Less-Nice Ned said.

Duncan had given her her present the day before, delivered by messenger. Of course, the cook had been the messenger, coming with the little wrapped box in his bike basket, crossing paths with Olinda the Boring Dog Walker, flirting with her, in her deep-cut tank shirt and shorts with the peace sign on the back pockets. Still, she'd never considered the possibility that the cook might have replied, 'Olinda.'

'You stop hovering like bees around the nest and get yourselves something to drink,' Duncan said to all the people suddenly grouped in front of them. Then he plopped down beside her. Duncan was eighty. He went to the gym two days a week and power-walked on the sidewalk by the beach another couple of nights. He had a droopy eye, but nothing was going to fix that. It wasn't even entirely age-related. When the bees scattered, he patted her knee lightly, through peaks and gulleys of fabric. 'And if you could have anything you wanted, what would it be?'

'Are you mad that I asked him?' she said.

'No, dear. He's not quite at the cut-off age where it would only be condescending. He's turned his life around since his incarceration, we see that. If he doesn't kill me in my sleep, or something. I've promised him money when I die, and he doesn't want to go back to prison and he doesn't seem violent, anyway. You know, they caught him because he peed a little during the robbery. How they cross-match pee, I don't know. Or maybe it was a hair that finally did him in.'

She started laughing. Her eyes darted to the cook, who was standing talking to her grandson and another man who'd entered the party but not come over to say hello. No, wait: it was Olinda. Olinda, in one of those trilbies everybody wore, pulled down low, and black leather motorcycle pants and black boots, her eyebrows drawn on darkly, her hair jaggedly cut off. As short a haircut as a man would have! And a black leather jacket to complete the outfit. Olinda raised a Heineken bottle in greeting.

Then, suddenly, because it was the same every year, an even larger crowd of people rushed in like a huge wave that would grow more and more threatening, more and more abstract, the higher it rose. You'd expect unwavering, nearly naked men and women with their feet spread for perfect balance to be riding it on surfboards until the enormous wave crested (which would have to be at the ceiling beams) and propelled everyone in her direction all at once, like so many grains of sand, toward where she sat like Neptune without a sceptre (without even a drink, publically) on a throne propped up with the Yellow Pages and hardback dictionaries you couldn't give away anymore. She was their destination, no different than arriving at the Pyramids, hardly distinguishable (except for her age) from the Fountain of Youth.

She crossed her legs. Her calves were gnarled varicose veins of seaweed. She'd started out in life the proud sandcastle fortress; she'd become the unlovely sun-bleached towel; she'd been so, so long ago the little shoe left behind; her finger was now the remaining claw of the crab that had already been pecked apart by seagulls.

'Merry Christmas, merry Christmas!'

An echo, or just a lot of identical thoughts? Impossible to tell, underwater, when you'd lost your sense of hearing and the sound inside your head was a roar.

Was it true that if you went under for the third time, that was it? Were only bird feathers – there! What about bird feathers? – didn't they repel water and float?

But too many garments . . . too much material . . . like shoes, they'd drag you down.

The word *money* popped up like a bit of the ocean's detritus riding in on a wave, but her lips formed the words 'Merry Christmas'. ■

NATURE MORTE

Helge Skodvin

Introduction by Audrey Niffenegger

The first piece of taxidermy I ever bought was an overstuffed toad. It cost twenty-five cents and it was somewhat broken; wires protruded where its hands should have been. I bought it on a whim, at a garage sale. Thirty years later, I still have it sitting on my desk, staring at me with its dull fake eyes.

The room where I write is full of taxidermy and books. They inhabit the shelves together: books on natural history, travel, antique medical textbooks and dictionaries make a habitat for a squirrel, a raccoon, a fox, various birds, a small rabbit, a rat from New York and a Chinese cat skeleton someone put together with a glue gun.

I feel sorry for each of these animals. They are banged up, dented, incompetently stuffed. They are not themselves.

I write at night, and the taxidermied animals ought to make eerie companions, but I hardly notice them. They have been here for years and each one has its place, incongruous but familiar. They only seem strange when someone new visits and sees them with fresh eyes.

In May 2015, Helge Skodvin took photographs of the World Taxidermy and Fish Carving Championships in Springfield, Missouri, a trade show for taxidermists. There are prizes, including a Lifetime Achievement Award. It is an event that offers many opportunities to see strangeness even in its most accomplished presentations, but Skodvin has turned his camera toward the casual awkwardness and unintentional surrealism that surround even the slickest showmanship. These photographs have the deadpan vibe of suburbia, nothing violent or unpleasant is happening and yet each photograph radiates melancholy. Helge Skodvin has caught the absurd menace and pity of the whole shebang. He confronts us with our hubris and our appetite for kitsch. Taxidermy is worrisome. Each kindly deer head, snarling leopard and elephant-foot umbrella stand is a place where our human contradictions converge. A piece of taxidermy was once an animal and that animal had memories and preferences. Once it has become a piece of taxidermy, it has nothing. The former animal is now an object. But this object causes us pain, because we know that stuffing it is profoundly incorrect. Even the most artful taxidermy is uncanny because the animal is out of context. Whether it is in a convention center or my bookcase, it looks wrong. We are thrilled and embarrassed to see the animal captured so far from its natural state.

Humans often don't want to let go of things and so we have developed techniques for keeping them always with us. Pickled specimens in jars, flowers pressed between the pages of books, snippets of hair in lockets, bronzed baby shoes, high-school yearbooks, cryonically preserved heads, vinyl records, frozen peas in the back of the freezer – we imagine that we might need these things later, in a week, a month, a century; we take comfort in the knowledge that we have preserved the past, it is not lost to us.

Taxidermy and photography share certain powers: they can stop time, simulate nature, grant us proximity to beings that want nothing to do with us. We can gaze at Helge Skodvin's photographs for as long as we like. He brings us to the edges of the action, where the illusion is thinnest, where the banal and the sublime are thrown together for a moment that extends into forever on the page.

Nature has secrets. We imagine that we can discover them if we look carefully enough, if we can take nature apart and reassemble it. We want to be close to nature and yet we are becoming more unnatural with every passing day. We are apart from nature and taxidermy is a reminder that time is passing and no matter how convincingly we reassemble the form, the ghost in the machine is gone for good. No matter how lifelike art might be, it cannot be alive. Taxidermy can be terribly moving, but mostly it is pathetic and even the pathetic fallacy is not enough to make it seem okay.

These are uncomfortable photographs. Helge Skodvin presents us to ourselves as destroyers and preservers, busily creating facsimiles of life from death. I suspect that the best thing to do might be to take all the taxidermy and burn it, sending the animals back to nature in the form of carbon and letting the past recede into the past. But for now these photographs preserve the indignities we visit upon nature, one elephant-foot umbrella stand at a time. ∎

Same magazine, different format

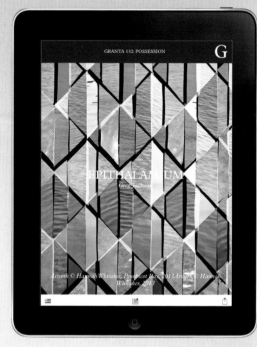

New app out now

GRANTA.COM

GRANTA

THE MAGAZINE OF NEW WRITING

PRINT SUBSCRIPTION REPLY FORM FOR UK, EUROPE
AND REST OF THE WORLD (includes digital and app access).
For digital-only subscriptions (includes app access), please visit granta.com/subscriptions.

GUARANTEE: If I am ever dissatisfied with my *Granta* subscription, I will simply notify you, and you will send me a complete refund or credit my credit card, as applicable, for all un-mailed issues.

YOUR DETAILS

TITLE ....

NAME ....

ADDRESS ....

POSTCODE ....

EMAIL ....

☐ Please tick this box if you do not wish to receive special offers from *Granta*
☐ Please tick this box if you do not wish to receive offers from organisations selected by *Granta*

YOUR PAYMENT DETAILS

1) ☐ Pay £32 (saving £20) by direct debit

To pay by direct debit please complete the mandate and return to the address shown below.

2) Pay by cheque or credit/debit card. Please complete below:

1 year subscription: ☐ UK: £36 ☐ Europe: £42 ☐ Rest of World: £46

3 year subscription: ☐ UK: £99 ☐ Europe: £108 ☐ Rest of World: £126

I wish to pay by ☐ CHEQUE ☐ CREDIT/DEBIT CARD

Cheque enclosed for £_____ made payable to *Granta*.

Please charge £_____ to my: ☐ Visa ☐ MasterCard ☐ Amex ☐ Switch/Maestro

Card No. ☐☐☐☐☐☐☐☐☐☐☐☐☐☐☐☐☐☐☐

Valid from *(if applicable)* ☐☐ / ☐☐   Expiry Date ☐☐ / ☐☐   Issue No. ☐☐

Security No. ☐☐☐

SIGNATURE .... DATE ....

Instructions to your Bank or Building Society to pay by direct debit

BANK NAME ....

BANK ADDRESS ....

POSTCODE ....

ACCOUNT IN THE NAMES(S) OF: ....

SIGNED .... DATE ....

DIRECT Debit

Instructions to your Bank or Building Society: Please pay Granta Publications direct debits from the account detailed on this instruction subject to the safeguards assured by the direct debit guarantee. I understand that this instruction may remain with Granta and, if so, details will be passed electronically to my bank/building society. Banks and building societies may not accept direct debit instructions from some types of account.

Bank/building society account number

☐☐☐☐☐☐☐☐

Sort Code

☐☐ ☐☐ ☐☐

Originator's Identification

9 1 3 1 3 3

Please mail this order form with payment instructions to:

Granta Publications
12 Addison Avenue
London, W11 4QR
Or call +44(0)208 955 7011 Or visit
GRANTA.COM/SUBSCRIPTIONS for details

"Raw, unnerving, and morbidly funny." —*Esquire*

"Immediately captivating."
—*The New Yorker*

"Irresistible."
—*The New York Times*

OUT NOW IN PAPERBACK FROM

McSWEENEY'S

STORE.MCSWEENEYS.NET

Sellafield, 2015.
Courtesy of the author

THE LEGACY

Fred Pearce

Not many people visit the Grey Croft stone circle in western Cumbria. The ten chest-high stones between the mountains of the Lake District and the waters of the Irish Sea have been there for five thousand years. And down the hill, across a field and over a small stream, lies Britain's largest industrial site, the Sellafield nuclear complex.

Sellafield is Britain's nuclear nightmare. It harbours the lethal remains of bomb-making, the accumulated radioactive waste from sixty years of nuclear electricity generation and the world's largest stockpile of plutonium. There is no other place on earth containing so much radioactive material in so confined an area.

I visited the stones first, before walking the double line of high razor-wire fences that surround the works. I was soon stopped by a squad car of the Civil Nuclear Constabulary, a dedicated armed force protecting nuclear installations. Nobody is taking any chances. The nuclear waste of Sellafield will remain dangerous for far longer than the Grey Croft stones have been here. The open-air ponds of radioactive sludge and corroded nuclear fuel, the tanks of hot liquid waste from nuclear reprocessing, the potentially explosive remains inside the sealed sarcophagus from a fire in 1957: all have radioactive half-lives measured in tens of thousands of years. A terrorist attack, earthquake or cataclysmic accident at Sellafield could make a large area of northern England uninhabitable.

Having satisfied the nuclear police that I posed no threat, I walked down a quiet country lane to Ponsonby Church, part of an estate that William the Conqueror gave to the Ponsonby family over nine hundred years ago. Lambs cavorted round the churchyard in the bright sun, as they must have done every spring, for centuries. But the new landlord here is the Nuclear Decommissioning Authority, and the manor house nearby is occupied by nuclear-waste engineers. Inside the church, a notice warns that if the Sellafield siren blows, nobody should leave. The doors should be shut and news sought by tuning into a radio.

I had travelled here to reacquaint myself with the radiology and psychogeography of Sellafield and its western Cumbrian hinterland. Sellafield and I go back a long way. When I worked as an editor at *New Scientist* in the early 1980s, it was still known as Windscale, and its leaks, accidents and scandals made regular copy. Since then, the headlines have dried up. You may think that this is because the nuclear beast has been tamed – that new management methods and health and safety rules, brought in to replace Cold War paranoia and hastily invented engineering, might have made Cumbria safe – but Sellafield harbours a toxic legacy of waste that is more dangerous than ever, as many of the buildings, once shiny and new, are now fractured and leaking. Weeds grow from the cracks. Inside, I found that the engineers, in their macho way, are proud that they superintend the two most hazardous industrial buildings in Western Europe; that making the place safe will cost over 70 billion pounds; that it will take a century or more to do. My journey outside the fences, however, revealed a second, equally corrosive legacy – of duplicity, secrecy and plain lies. That legacy may be just as hard to clean.

From its first days, Windscale was steeped in the subterfuge arising from a secret project to rescue Britain from humiliation in the days after the Second World War. British scientists had worked with their American counterparts at Los Alamos in New Mexico to develop the atomic bomb. Then in 1946, wishing to keep the bomb to themselves as the Cold War developed, the US Congress banned American scientists from sharing nuclear secrets with their British colleagues. Outraged, Prime Minister Clement Attlee ordered the banished scientists – headed by Britain's 'man behind the mushroom cloud', the diffident, state-educated mathematics prodigy William Penney – to start from scratch and build a British bomb.

Bankrupt Britain put vast resources into the project. The weapons were assembled at Aldermaston in Berkshire, while a site on the remote Cumbrian coastline was chosen to manufacture the plutonium. Two primitive nuclear reactors, known as the Windscale Piles, were built by the River Calder. Their thick concrete walls contained thousands of tonnes of graphite, honeycombed with horizontal channels to house slugs of uranium metal sheathed in aluminium cans.

Packed together, the uranium emitted sufficient neutrons to start a nuclear chain reaction, turning some of it into plutonium. Meanwhile, the graphite prevented the reactions from running out of control. The uranium slugs were then pushed out of the back of the pile into a giant, open-air pond to cool, before going to the reprocessing plant, where the fuel was dissolved in nitric acid to release the plutonium. The reactions inside the piles created huge amounts of waste heat, which future reactor designs would use to generate electricity. But these piles were intended only to manufacture plutonium. Air pumped through the graphite core took the heat up the two 120-metre chimneys, where filters captured any radioactive particles.

So far so good. Using what they remembered from Los Alamos, Penney's scientists delivered the first plutonium to Aldermaston in early 1952. Two months later, the first British atomic bomb was detonated on a ship near the Montebello Islands off Western Australia. By then, however, the US had detonated a much bigger and more sophisticated weapon, the hydrogen bomb, whose design employed secrets no British scientists knew.

Penney's team were given a new job: to make an H-bomb. That

proved much harder. But in the aftermath of the Suez Crisis of 1956, the new prime minister, Harold Macmillan, believed such a bomb was essential to rebuilding Britain's global clout and bolstering relations with the US, especially atomic cooperation. Without such a device, a Cabinet paper in June 1957 argued, Britain would be 'virtually knocked out as a nuclear power'.

When an H-bomb proved beyond Britain's best atomic scientists, Macmillan led them to indulge in what Norman Dombey, the researcher who exposed the lie in 1992, would call a 'thermonuclear bluff'. They hatched a secret plan to test a giant A-bomb, masquerading as an H-bomb. But that required much more plutonium. Windscale went flat out. Corners were cut. Safety was sacrificed. Remembering events much later for a BBC programme, John Dunworth of the nuclear research laboratory at Harwell, one of those who had warned of the dangers at the time, said: 'They were running much too close to the precipice.' The scene was set for the world's first major nuclear accident.

In the summer of 1957, under intense pressure to manufacture more plutonium, operators kept postponing downtime needed to cleanse the piles of Wigner energy in the core. This energy built up as the bombardment of neutrons displaced atoms in the graphite. It could cause a fire unless it was released by operators shutting down the nuclear reactions and then gradually heating the reactor core.

The long-postponed Wigner release finally began on 9 October. Jittery operators, working without a manual and anxious to get the reactor back into production, added too much heat too quickly. One of the fuel cans burst and the uranium inside it released even more heat, igniting a fire that spread through the pile. The uranium was ablaze and before long radioactive smoke had overwhelmed the filter and began pouring out of the chimney.

There was panic. Managers press-ganged off-duty workers who were watching a film at the works cinema in nearby Seascale and gave them scaffolding poles to push jammed fuel cans out of their channels and away from the burning pile. One young scientist, Morlais Harris, told me that he was sent to monitor equipment on top of the reactor, where managers trying to control the fire forgot about him for sixteen hours before bringing him down after the fire was put out. Workers in the know – there was no official information, and many had no idea of the risks – called their families living nearby and told them to flee.

With the fire still spreading, the pile's managers decided to douse the fire with water. This was do or die. They knew that spraying water onto the burning, molten core risked causing an explosion. 'Cumberland would have been finished. It would have been like Chernobyl,' site foreman Cyril McManus told interviewers recently for an oral history of Sellafield. But the water worked. After three days, the fire was out.

The government asked Penney to report on how the fire had happened, but his findings of the chaotic management at Windscale were so damning that Macmillan recalled every copy. The report was only released to the public under the thirty-year rule in January 1988. Instead, Macmillan issued a statement that blamed the fire on an 'error of judgement' over the Wigner energy release by an unnamed rogue worker. No mention was made of the underlying cause – government demands for ever more plutonium. 'He covered it up, plain and simple,' Macmillan's grandson and biographer, Lord Stockton, later told the BBC.

In the immediate aftermath of the fire, radiologists monitoring what went up the pile chimney said the main risk to the public was radioactive iodine falling on Cumbrian pastures and getting into milk. Over a couple of weeks, two million litres of milk were collected from farms and poured down drains into the Irish Sea. Managers said this was 'erring wildly on the cautious side' against a 'theoretical' risk, but they were clearly worried. Secretly, in the weeks afterwards, they sent McManus and others as far away as Devon, collecting samples of soil and vegetation to check the spread of the fallout.

Decades later, it emerged that iodine was not the most dangerous component of cloud. It also contained polonium, an element so radioactive it glows blue in the dark, and though a handful of scientists were aware of this, it was hushed up. A few specks are enough to kill, as former Russian agent Alexander Litvinenko discovered when someone dropped polonium in his tea in a London hotel in 2006.

Polonium was the essential trigger at the heart of the British bomb, and it was being produced in the Windscale Piles by irradiating bismuth. But this was top secret. The Americans no longer used polonium in their bombs, and revealing that Britain still did would have shown how backward British bomb-makers were. Because of this, its lethal presence in the cloud was never mentioned in any assessments of the radiological hazard from the fire at the time. A few British atomic scientists knew enough of polonium's presence to mention it fleetingly in a paper presented to a UN technical conference the year after the fire, but the implications were apparently not understood by those conducting risk assessments, and the presence of polonium in the cloud was forgotten for thirty-five years.

Only in 1983 did environmental activist and Newcastle University librarian John Urquhart stumble on the long-forgotten reference and bring his findings to *New Scientist*. Our scoop was subsequently confirmed by government radiologists, who said they too had been kept in the dark. They calculated the likely death toll from the polonium at about seventy, making it probably the main cause of deaths from the cloud. Nobody has ever assessed the additional risk to workers trying to contain the fire.

Some may argue that the fire was a price worth paying. It forced the closure of the Windscale Piles, but they had by then produced enough plutonium for the successful test of a giant A-bomb masquerading as an H-bomb, which persuaded Congress to rescind the ban on cooperative nuclear research and to allow Eisenhower and Macmillan, by now close friends, to resume what is still known today as the 'special relationship' between the two countries. Ever since the signing of the 1958 US-UK Mutual Defence Agreement, British scientists have been able to access US bomb-making expertise and buy American bombs. 'Our armed forces have never used entirely

British-designed weapons,' Dombey told me. 'In 1958, we built and tested H-bombs, but they were never put into service. They were too big.' In truth, the purpose of the bluff was always more diplomatic than technical – to secure Britain's place on the UN Security Council and in Washington as a nuclear power.

But the fire has scarred Windscale's reputation ever since. The cover-up – and Macmillan's decision to blame it on young operators who had risked their lives to prevent much worse – undermined faith in the project and in its management. The narrative of Windscale, and subsequently of Sellafield, as an alien, dangerous and duplicitous presence on the Cumbrian coast was set.

Despite the fire, Windscale remained in business. In 1956, the Queen had opened new, more sophisticated reactors just metres from the piles. The Calder Hall reactors also initially manufactured plutonium for bombs, but their primary purpose was to generate electricity. The cooling gas – now carbon dioxide rather than air – was captured, and its heat was used to drive conventional power-station turbines. The reactors became the prototypes for a fleet of Magnox reactors across Britain. Nuclear energy, Britons were told in the 1960s, would be 'too cheap to meter'. In 1971, the old quasi-military UK Atomic Energy Authority (UKAEA) was replaced at Windscale by British Nuclear Fuels Limited (BNFL), whose task was to commercialise nuclear power.

It was a brave new world, but the culture of secrecy and cover-ups persisted. It created not just a climate of fear, but also a landscape of secrets. To chart its contours, I recently met Martin Forwood, who runs Cumbrians Opposed to a Radioactive Environment (CORE). Soft-spoken and bearded, Forwood is a former soldier, policeman and government scientist. He took me on his 'alternative tour' of Sellafield's hinterland.

We started on the banks of the River Esk near the hamlet of Newbiggin, about ten kilometres from Sellafield. Forwood got a Geiger counter out of the car and headed for the tidal salt marshes.

The counter began to click. There were radioactive particles beneath our feet. The surface mud showed three or four times the natural background level. Then, as he pointed his counter at mud a few inches down on the exposed riverbank, the clicking accelerated to a mad chatter at around thirty times the natural level.

The buried mud was seriously radioactive. 'Livestock graze here,' Forwood said. Fishermen dig for bait; people pick samphire, a local culinary delicacy; and a few metres away the Cumbria Coastal Way offers a shortcut through the mud at low tide. But there were no warning signs. 'There could be particles of plutonium and americium on my boots,' he said as we returned to the car. In theory, his boots should probably have gone for burial in the concrete-lined trenches for low-level radioactive waste at Sellafield's dump at nearby Drigg. 'But you get similar readings all along the coast here,' Forwood said. 'You can't remove the whole of the Cumbrian shoreline.'

In 2005, Forwood's CORE colleagues campaigning against Italian nuclear waste coming to Sellafield decided to bake a Cumbrian pizza topped with Esk mud and samphire. They handed it to the economic consul at the Italian embassy in London, with a warning note. He called in the Environment Agency, which took the radioactive pizza to the atomic labs at Harwell in Oxfordshire where it was quarantined for eight years before being interred at Drigg in 2013.

Most of the radioactive particles in the mud come, of course, from Sellafield. They had been discharged down the works' two-kilometre pipeline into the Irish Sea. Marjorie Higham, a Sellafield scientist in the early days, told the oral-history project that her managers assured her that 'the plutonium [would] adhere to the mud at the bottom of the sea in perpetuity. But of course it didn't. It moves around.' Some of it washes back on the tides that scour the coast. It turns up on beaches and gets trapped in the silt.

Routine discharges down the pipe are legal, but the oral history is full of stories about unwanted and highly radioactive liquids being secretly poured down the pipe. Occasionally the perpetrators get caught. Shortly after midnight in November 1983, half a tonne of reprocessing solvent went into the Irish Sea. This illegal discharge created a radioactive slick that floated ashore. Some Greenpeace activists happened to be diving close to the outlet at the time, devising plans to block it, and they came to the surface with their Geiger counters in overdrive. The discharge, which might otherwise have gone unnoticed, became front-page news and the local beaches were closed for six months. BNFL ended up with a court conviction and a £10,000 fine.

The lower levels of radioactivity that Forwood's Geiger counter finds in recently deposited surface mud show that the pipeline's radioactive discharges are generally a lot less than they once were. But the higher levels below the surface reveal that past pollution hasn't gone away.

How dangerous is this? A cluster of cases of leukaemia among children living around Sellafield in the 1970s and 80s raised alarms that have never subsided. First revealed by a Yorkshire TV documentary in 1983, the cluster was later confirmed by government epidemiologists, who found leukaemia rates fourteen times the national average. Alan Postlethwaite, a local vicar when the scare was at its height, told the Sellafield oral-history project that 'within quite a short period of time, I conducted funerals of three children who died of leukaemia'. Statisticians had told him to 'expect one in twenty years, and we'd had three in twelve months . . . That put the frighteners on us.'

BNFL blamed the cluster on outside workers bringing a mystery virus to a previously isolated community. That is plausible, though no virus has ever been identified. A major study funded by BNFL in 2002 found that the children of Sellafield workers who had been exposed to radiation in the plant's early years were twice as likely as the national average to develop leukaemia.

The cluster seems to have disappeared more recently. But fears run deep. When one couple living in a house overlooking the Esk Estuary tested the contents of their vacuum cleaner, they found plutonium, americium and caesium levels thousands of times higher than natural background levels. And a culture of cover-ups breeds fear and anger, which often gets directed against those who upset the status quo. When the couple brought a case against BNFL for damages, locals stopped visiting the village post office they ran, and someone superglued their front door shut. They sold up and left the area.

Forwood and I stopped at a guest house on a cliff outside Seascale. In the house next door, he told me, two sisters, Jane and Barrie Robinson, ran a bird sanctuary in the garden until a test in 1998 revealed that many of the birds were dangerously radioactive. It turned out the birds often roosted in contaminated buildings at Sellafield and may have fed on insects living around its open-air fuel storage ponds. Soon after, the authorities put 1,500 radioactive bird corpses into lead canisters for burial at Drigg, along with topsoil, garden plants and even the sisters' garden gnomes.

Sellafield has a history of showing a cavalier attitude to its neighbours. A scientist at the works, Frank Leslie, turned whistle-blower after the 1957 fire and told the *Manchester Guardian* about a reckless safety culture in which regular discharges of radioactivity into the air over Cumbria had been hushed up – something BNFL finally admitted in 1986. Similarly in the early days, highly radioactive junk was put into the Drigg trenches as casually as if it were household trash going into a municipal dump.

The safety culture was no better inside the plant. A few weeks after the 1983 beach contamination, it emerged that the plant laundry's managers had adjusted alarms meant to alert staff to radioactivity on overalls to make sure they 'did not go off too often'. And then a broken valve in the reprocessing works released a plutonium mist that exposed eleven workers to serious contamination. Around that time, says McManus, workers often accumulated so much radiation in their bodies that they were banned from working in contaminated areas for the rest of their days. He was among those who became, as he puts it, 'radiation lepers'.

For many years, Sellafield ran a secret programme of autopsies on former workers to check for radioactivity. I stumbled on this one day in 1986, when I was leafing through the journal of the government's National Radiological Protection Board. The board's medical researcher Don Popplewell described how the plutonium in the lungs and lymph nodes of Cumbrian corpses were at much higher levels than those in corpses in the rest of the country. The findings were reported without discussing the means employed to get them which were, as Don Popplewell told me, technically illegal. Analysing corpses for 'scientific' reasons, rather than to ascertain the cause of death, was common practice at the time. In a handful of former Sellafield workers the plutonium levels were hundreds, and in one case thousands, of times higher than normal. When I called Popplewell he told me that Sellafield's chief medical officer, Geoffrey Schofield, had analysed more than fifty corpses of former workers and found yet higher levels. All this was done even though, as I wrote in *New Scientist*, it was 'strictly illegal to examine autopsy tissue except to ascertain the cause of death'.

My article sank without a trace until twenty years later when, after an unconnected scandal over illegal autopsies on children in Liverpool, lawyers turned it up. They raised a stink and an inquiry was held into the Sellafield autopsies. The government duly issued an apology in 2010, and Schofield was disgraced (they even took his name off the front of a building on a Cumbrian science park), but strangely the staggering contamination of Sellafield workers found by Schofield and Popplewell has been quietly forgotten.

Most people I spoke to during my journeys around Sellafield told me that whatever the worries about historical environmental contamination, the real hazards from the works lie inside the fences, and they are not going away. So I arranged a tour.

The most important buildings on the site are the two vast reprocessing complexes. Reprocessing spent fuel from reactors, mostly from external sources but also its own, has been Sellafield's *raison d'être* since it opened. In the old days, it was done to extract the plutonium necessary to make bombs, and more recently the output has been earmarked for the manufacture of new fuel to be put back into reactors. This idea of recycling nuclear fuel, thus optimising energy production, has always been the dream of nuclear engineers.

The spent fuel comes to Sellafield from distant nuclear power stations by train in crash-proof flasks, which are placed into cooling ponds drenched in millions of litres of water taken each day from a lake inside the Lake District National Park. The fuel is then dissolved in nitric acid to separate out the potentially reusable elements. Finally, these valuable products are put into store, while the hot, acidic and extremely radioactive 'high-level liquid waste' is collected in giant stainless-steel tanks, each twice the size of a large shipping container, ready to be concentrated in evaporators and then sealed in glass for eventual burial, a process called vitrification.

Two plants do all this. Both have been hit by repeated shutdowns and backlogs. The Magnox Reprocessing Plant takes spent fuel from the country's ageing Magnox reactors, which are now mostly closed, and spent Magnox fuel needs to be reprocessed within a year. If it is left too long in cooling ponds, the fuel rods corrode, releasing radioactive material into the water. This has happened in the past, most dramatically during the coal miners' strikes of the early 1970s, when nuclear power stations were run as hard as possible to keep the lights on, and Sellafield was overwhelmed with spent fuel. It happened again during a six-week strike at Sellafield itself in 1977, which shut down all reprocessing. The resulting mess of unprocessed spent fuel is a continuing problem that will require a multi-billion-dollar clean-up operation to solve.

A second plant, the Thermal Oxide Reprocessing Plant (THORP), handles so-called oxide fuels from Britain's later generation of advanced gas-cooled reactors (AGRs) and the pressurised water reactors more common worldwide. THORP was Sellafield's great hope in the days of BNFL, from the 1970s to the 1990s. The company wanted Sellafield to become the world centre for reprocessing. It would take spent fuel from around the world and convert it into new fuel, generating huge revenues for the government.

But from the day it opened in 1994, THORP's commercial rationale has evaporated. Enthusiasm for nuclear power has waned and with it demand for the new fuel. What's more, unlike spent Magnox fuel, the modern feedstock for THORP can be stored for decades without deteriorating, so the plant's value as a waste-disposal facility has been minimal. Since it opened for business in 1994, the intended big moneymaker has become what Harold Bolter, BNFL's PR man during the inquiry and company secretary when it was being built, later called 'a huge financial drain on the nation'.

The plant has continued to work, though never reliably. Constant stops and starts have created backlogs of spent fuel in the cooling ponds, while delays in investing in the evaporation and vitrification plant have led to a build-up of high-level liquid waste. According to Gordon Thompson of the Institute for Resource and Security Studies in the US, the tanks of waste contain many times more radioactive caesium than was released across Europe during the Chernobyl disaster in Ukraine in 1986. A worst-case accident at Sellafield could release 90 per cent of it, he says.

The prospects of such a disaster may be remote, but it could happen swiftly if the tanks were breached by an act of terrorism or an earthquake, or if the cooling coils failed. According to a Royal Commission report on Britain's nuclear industry as long ago as 1976, a cooling failure would 'cause the solution to boil dry and the heat generated would then disseminate volatile materials to the atmosphere and cause widespread contamination'. If that happened, says Thompson, 'a large area of land could be rendered unusable for a period of decades. Neighbouring countries could be significantly affected.' He estimates there would be three thousand cancer deaths.

Such an event has long been of concern to nuclear regulators. In 2001, the Health and Safety Executive ordered Sellafield to cut stocks of the liquid waste from 1,575 cubic metres to no more than 200 cubic metres by 2015, either by speeding up evaporation and vitrification or by halting reprocessing. But in January of this year, as the target date arrived and the last-reported stockpile still stood at 900 cubic metres, the HSE's successor, the Office for Nuclear Regulation, abandoned the target.

It is hard to see a case for such lenience. Post-9/11, the possibility of a terrorist attack on Sellafield must have increased, and a reassessment of seismic risks, made after the earthquake that wrecked Japan's Fukushima Daiichi Nuclear Power Plant, resulted in the government extending the zone around Sellafield covered by evacuation plans from two to six kilometres earlier this year.

But the new regulator has decided that operational convenience takes priority. The target became a problem for Sellafield's managers because of continuing gridlock in handling the liquid waste: a new £640 million evaporator promised for completion in 2010 is still more than a year off, and the plant that encapsulates the liquid into glass has suffered a series of shutdowns. Rather than halting reprocessing, the regulator has decided to let the radioactive build-up continue.

This is typical. Sellafield has a lamentable history of management failures that create backlogs of waste and allows them to accumulate in unsafe conditions. The 'legacy problem', as managers call it, became so great that in 2005 the government replaced the bankrupt 'commercial' BNFL with the Nuclear Decommissioning Authority (NDA), whose top priority is to work out how to shut Sellafield down and make the site safe for future generations – something even optimists believe will take upwards of a century.

On my tour of the works, my NDA hosts were keen to show me their highest-profile decommission to date. I watched as robots scooped up the last remains from the floor of the prototype Windscale AGR reactor, leaving behind its iconic golf-ball exterior. Much of the waste has gone into 120 concrete boxes, each two metres high, stacked in a store close by. The boxes are so safe that I took up their offer to go and touch them. This technical success has proved expensive, however. The dismantling of the Windscale AGR reactor, which was intended to take six years, ended up taking twenty years and costing £111 million.

Altogether, Sellafield has 240 radioactive buildings awaiting decommissioning. The most obvious is the pile that caught fire almost sixty years ago. Every day, Sellafield's 10,000 workers still pass the remains – nobody has yet dared breach the seal. Inside, the graphite core still contains the Wigner energy that operators were trying to remove on the fateful day of the fire. Disturbing the remains could cause the core and the estimated fifteen tonnes of buckled uranium fuel to catch fire again, or even explode.

The pile will wait its turn. There are four other buildings that the NDA says have higher priority. Each will take billions of pounds to make safe. They contain fuel and waste that should have been made safe decades ago, but were instead abandoned. They are the dark hearts of Sellafield, the radioactive reminders of past follies.

The structure known as B29 was one of Windscale's first. The hundred-metre-long open-air pond sits like an outsize swimming pool between the remains of the two Windscale piles. It received the cans of spent fuel as they were pushed from the backs of the piles, prior to reprocessing. After the 1957 fire, it was retired, but it was resurrected as an emergency store for spent fuel during the miners' strikes of the early 1970s, when Sellafield's reprocessing line couldn't keep up. Stuck there too long, the skips of fuel began to corrode and the pond and its contents were abandoned again. The fuel remains and the corrosion has created 300 cubic metres of radioactive sludge that coats the bottom of the pond.

Close by is B41. This giant silo, constructed in 1950, houses six hoppers, each twenty-one metres high, which received the aluminium cans cut from pile fuel after it left B29. Later, it took cladding that sheathed spent Magnox fuel. Once full, it was closed in 1965. Plans for emptying it in the 1990s came to nothing. As the cans and cladding corrode, they generate hydrogen that could catch fire; argon gas is constantly pumped in to stifle any conflagration.

B30 opened in 1959. It is another giant pond, 150 metres long, and like its older brother B29 it is open to the elements. Until 1985, it received spent Magnox fuel awaiting reprocessing. As with B29, it still contains fuel that stayed too long and has corroded. The 1,500 cubic metres of sludge and corroded fuel in the pond contain up to 1.3 tonnes of plutonium. Sellafield managers don't show B30 to visitors, but pictures leaked in 2014 revealed weeds growing round the tank and radioactive algae on the water. B30 is known to workers as 'dirty 30', because since the 1980s it has been Sellafield's biggest source of contamination. They can only work in some areas for two or three minutes at a time. Safety experts call it Western Europe's most hazardous industrial building.

The second most dangerous industrial building in Western Europe is B38, just next door. After B41 was filled, its four concrete silos took cladding from Magnox reactors. Some of the waste has since liquefied and sludge has seeped through cracks in the floor, forming a radioactive plume spreading through the soil beneath. As with B41, there is a risk of explosion from the hydrogen being generated in the silos, which are constantly ventilated.

The first steps towards emptying these monstrous ponds and silos have finally been taken, though all is not going well. This spring, the NDA postponed the expected completion dates for emptying B29 and B41 by five years, to 2030 and 2029 respectively, and the schedules may well slip further. 'We have to do a lot of Research and Development just to characterise the inventory before we can work out how to retrieve the materials,' Paul Howarth, the managing director of the UK National Nuclear Laboratory told me as we toured the site.

Sellafield's baleful inventory also includes the world's largest stockpile of non-military plutonium – over 120 tonnes of the stuff, with around four tonnes added from reprocessing each year. That is more than the US and Russian civilian stockpiles put together, and enough to make 20,000 Nagasaki-size bombs. A quarter of it is owned by foreign countries, mostly Japan and Germany, that sent spent fuel to the UK for reprocessing, but few are interested in taking it back.

The original purpose of separating the plutonium was to make fuel for a future generation of reactors, and many believe that project should be revived. The government's chief scientist for energy David MacKay says that it contains enough energy to run the country's electricity grid for five hundred years, but efforts to build two plutonium-burning plants – a fast-breeder reactor at Dounreay in Scotland and a mixed-oxide fuel plant at Sellafield – were both abandoned after the expenditure of more than a billion pounds. The asset has become a liability.

It is safe, if kept secure. But managers at Sellafield are reluctant even to identify the building containing the stuff, which costs around £100 million a year to protect. Most of the plutonium is in the form of plutonium dioxide powder that could be made into a crude nuclear bomb. In 2007, the Royal Society said the stockpile 'poses a severe security risk', and 'undermines the UK's credibility in non-proliferation debates'.

Whatever happens to the plutonium, the rest of Sellafield's lethal legacy has to be kept safe. Terrorism is one threat, but so are the societies of the future – people whose cultures and technical skills could be as far removed from ours as the Neolithic people who built the Grey Croft stone circle. And safety, almost everyone agrees, ultimately means burial deep underground.

A couple of kilometres from Sellafield's back fence, within metres of the Lake District National Park, lies the burial site the authorities keep coming back to. In the 1990s, Longlands Farm was proposed as the entry point for a test repository that might one day extend underground for up to twenty square kilometres. After a damning planning inspectors' report warned that the rocks could transmit radioactive leaks into water supplies, however, the government threw the plan out. But a decade on, new ministers revived it, only for the Cumbrian County Council to vote against it four years ago.

Eddie Martin, county leader at the time of the vote, thinks the government could be about to resurrect it once more. He now runs the Cumbria Trust, which is dedicated to preventing that from happening. When I met him at his home outside Maryport, he said: 'They want the disposal facility here not because the geology is favourable – it isn't, as the old miners know, it is riddled with faults and fissures that make it unsuitable – but because they think we won't object.'

Maybe policymakers in faraway London are right to think that. Western Cumbria is trapped by Sellafield. The complex provides most of the area's jobs, spends most of the money, and has its tentacles in all kinds of local activities. Even the current local MP Jamie Reed – who was returned in May with a 2,564 vote majority – is a former PR man at Sellafield. He is supported by GMB, the largest blue-collar union at the site. Sellafield's relatively high wages and environmental stigma repel other potential industrial employers, and school-leavers can either work at Sellafield or take low-paid work in tourism or farming. This summer, locals were being asked to comment on plans for a giant conventional nuclear power plant right over the fence from Sellafield. With many jobs on offer, they may be tempted. Construction could be under way by 2018.

Back in 1946, the government stipulated that, for safety reasons, Sellafield's plutonium factory should be at least fifty miles from any large town. 'Sellafield has stored the country's nuclear waste and operated some of its most dangerous plants for almost seventy years,' Eddie Martin tells me. 'For what we have done for the country, the streets should be paved with gold. Instead, we have been largely ignored. Our infrastructure is poor. Too many children live in poverty. And in the back of our mind, we know that if there is an accident the whole area could become uninhabitable.'

Continued political chaos doesn't help. In 2008, most of Sellafield's activities were privatised. The aim, said then energy minister Mike O'Brien, was to 'get to grips with the legacy after decades of inaction'. But as costs ballooned, O'Brien's successors decided to renationalise it in early 2015. Whoever is in charge, the bills keep going up, from half a billion pounds in 1980 to 79 billion pounds today. Unlike other nations that rely on nuclear power, Britain never established a special fund to pay for eventual decommissioning. As former energy minister Chris Huhne put it four years ago: 'When waste started piling up, we effectively crossed our fingers and hoped that it would all go away.' ∎

Travesty

By-catch of the ghost nets and onion sacks,
giant sea turtles paddled in makeshift tanks
recuperating with missing flippers or scored backs,
and I had brought us there on holiday, a sorry
pedagogical impulse. Dog is miffed, channeling
Sir Walter Raleigh: 'We found thousands of
Tortugas egs, which are very wholesome meate.'
We're told it's a she, but my youngest won't hear of it:
So I refer to *him*, the new tortoise. Secretly,
we have our tête-à-têtes; corked in her flask,
inquiring of the perimeter whether it might be
vulnerable somewhere, she stretches on her tippy toes,
a comedienne, but from another perspective,
the victim of a mythological punishment.

The bends of the Kanektok river in Quinhagak.

UPRIVER

Kathleen Jamie

Quinhagak is a Yup'ik village on the Yukon-Kuskokwim Delta in western Alaska. There, where the Bering Sea is rapidly eroding the coast, a remarkable archaeological dig is under way. Called 'Nunalleq', the site is an abandoned Yup'ik village dating from pre-contact times, five hundred years ago. It is yielding an astonishingly rich array of artefacts, and reawakening cultural awareness and confidence among the Yup'ik people. The site is being excavated by a team from Aberdeen University, with help and support from the Quinhagak community. Last year, thanks to funding from the Leverhulme Trust, I was able to join the archaeologists for the short digging season.

One Sunday, after we had been in Quinhagak about three weeks, Warren finally found the time to take us on our promised trip upriver. It's not that folk here don't love river trips – especially in August when the salmon are running, for the Kanektok is a famous salmon river – it's just that Warren was always busy. You want something done, we'd been told, you ask Warren Jones.

In his forties, burly by Yup'ik standards and rarely off his cell phone, Warren was president of the Quinhagak village corporation. Every day a succession of people traipse up the village hall stairs, looking to get things done. One morning I traipsed up there myself and found Warren sitting at a desk covered in forms and documents to do with grants and projects. With due deference, I told him I was a writer and, if possible, I'd like to discover something about Yup'ik life.

For a moment he lifted his gaze from the paper-strewn desk to look through the window at the miles of tundra in its summer greens. Then he said, 'Just tell 'em we don't live in igloos!'

Sunday was everyone's day off, so the trip became a family affair. Along with three of us from the dig came Warren, his son Patrick, his wife Jeanette and Teddi, Jeanette's sister. Both these women were petite, dark-haired and quietly competent. They tied their black hair back and, like the men, wore combat trousers, hoodies and ball caps. Teddi admitted she was very glad to be going outdoors. She was the manager of Quinhagak's substantial supermarket, which meant she spent her working days in a huge metal-clad shed without windows. As manager, she was responsible for ordering all the goods, and there wasn't much you couldn't buy in the store, all airfreighted in. Except alcohol, because Quinhagak is a dry village. Instead of booze, the small planes carry pallet-loads of sugary drinks. One day half a dozen coconuts appeared, which made me laugh. But then, I suppose a coconut in Quinhagak is no more odd than a coconut in Aberdeen.

To reach the boats we all piled into one of the town's few cars – a beat-up yellow station wagon – and drove about a mile and a half from the township to where the road ended at a series of gravel pits. Because the river had recently swept away a sizeable stretch of the road, we had to edge the car carefully around the margin which remained. The town's airstrip used to lie beside the river too, but that also had been swept away. Such are Warren's headaches. Another airstrip was soon built a mile farther inland, land being freely available. The delta's waterways have always been dynamic; its hundreds of square miles are riddled with melt pools, oxbows and creeks. The very name Quinhagak – or Kwinarraq – means 'new river channel'. What's alarming, the people say, is the scale and speed of recent changes. The Bering Sea is rising, the permafrost melting. When the permafrost melts, the earth falls apart and structures built on it collapse. High tides bring floods to the coastal villages and sweep away what little infrastructure they have.

The boats were grey, flat-bottomed metal skiffs with a ramped front and a square stern. There were many such boats around the village, tied up on muddy creeks; every family seemed to possess at least one. Because we were a party of seven, we split ourselves between two. Warren manned the first himself, standing next to the hefty outboard engine. Young Patrick drove the other. Of course, they took fishing rods. Of course, they took a powerful rifle, tucked away in the stern.

We hoped to reach the mountains forty miles upstream, so set off at high speed. Out on the quick river, Warren and Patrick's skill lay in putting their boats into the right channel, the best braid, in judging speed and cornering against the onrush as the river widened and narrowed. Hazards included half-submerged logs that had been swept down from forests in the distant interior, and the way the river looped right, then left. Every fleet-flowing bend was paired with a reef of grey shingle. Gulls flew up from these reefs as we neared. The riverbanks proper were at times dense with willow scrub, at times soft and peaty, and easily claimed by the scouring water. I sat in the front, trying to be vigilant, looking out for bears or moose or birds on the riverbanks, but the engines scared them away. Warren wore shades and ear protectors; it was too loud to speak.

Because it was salmon season we passed many fishermen standing on the gravel banks. These were big bearded men from the southern States, the Lower 48. The rivers they fished were on Yup'ik land, managed by Native community-owned corporations. They provided the services, stores, boats and camps, and took the fees. That was the deal. Solemnly, the fishermen waved as we zipped by. They were surprised, I think, not at the dark-haired Yup'ik women in the boats – they scoot upriver all the time, berry-picking or hunting – but at the three white women in their company. The fishing trips looked to be all male.

After some miles of headwind and river spray, Warren and Patrick slowed the boats and nudged them against one of the shingle beaches.

They could resist no longer: they had to catch fish. Teddi and Jeanette secured the boats with ropes and they wasted no time in assembling the fishing rods. I wandered off a few yards, stepping over a bear pat, brown and crusty. It was the diameter of a saucer and decorated with undigested red berries. A paw print with claws, not much smaller, was pressed into the silt nearby.

'Did you smell that bear back there?' asked Warren.

I'd seen him wrinkle his nose and point to the bushes of the riverbank, but hadn't understood.

Thinking the fishing would take ages, I hunkered on a washed-up log to wait. I looked at the grey shingle at my feet and a spray of yellow poppies in bloom among the stones. I kept an eye out for bears among the willow scrub on the bank opposite, and watched Teddi casting her line out into the river. The August air was not quite warm, not quite cold. Dark clouds were gathering and a breeze rising, the kind of breeze that precedes rain. I prepared myself to be bored, but within ten minutes Teddi and Warren had each landed a silvery coho salmon the length of my arm. The fish were smacked hard on the head with a stick and gutted at once with a deft movement of a knife, then stowed in a polythene bag. Out in the water further salmon twisted, trout too, all pushing and nudging up to their spawning grounds.

With the fish in the bag we made to leave, but first Jeanette shyly produced lollipops – a flat boiled-sweet kind I hadn't seen in years. The women sucked the lollies, the men smoked cigarettes, and then we pushed the boats out. The riverbanks began to swell higher, and in a mile or two more trees appeared, cottonwoods, releasing a dreamy autumnal smell. From time to time we passed beaver lodges. We turned a leftward bend and slowed because there was a bald eagle nest nearby, and sure enough, from one of the tall trees, an eagle took off at our approach. In a shallow we idled, watching as the bird made a wide loop overhead.

We listened for Patrick's boat. It didn't come. We waited some minutes more. Jeanette told us the Yup'ik name for the eagle, several equally stressed syllables I instantly forgot. Warren told us that cottonwood is favoured for making harpoons to hunt seals. We turned back downstream to see what was up, and found the second boat pulled up on a shingle bank strewn with bleached driftwood. Engine trouble. This was the reason Warren had wanted to take two boats: just in case. The river feels like a highway, but like a highway, as soon as you stop and silence falls, you feel the scale of the vast land around, its pressing strangeness, your exposure. At least I did. We hadn't seen any other boats or fishermen for a while.

Washed up on this bank were plenty of sticks, so as Warren and Patrick concentrated on the engine, Teddi and Jeanette set about making a windbreak. As with the fishing, they were quick of hand. First they gathered a few branches. They rammed these into the silt, wove more branches between and draped the frame with a blue plastic sheet. This we huddled under, because it was starting to rain. As they built a fire, I watched carefully. The sisters worked as a team, bent over with heads together, barely speaking because they didn't have to. They scooped out some gravel to make a shallow pit about a foot long. They filled the pit with dry grasses they'd gathered at the shore, then laid thin twigs over in a lattice. On top of that came bigger sticks. One lick of flame from Teddi's Zippo lighter and the fire caught.

Within fifteen minutes the sisters had provided shelter and heat. Now, they went scouting for fresh willow wands among the thickets behind the beach. These thickets were a haunt of bears; one didn't go alone. Even if we wanted to pee, we went in company. As the fire gained heat they whittled the willow wands with knives until they were sharp-pointed. Then, they took not the salmon but hot-dog sausages, and rammed them onto the sticks. Everyone hunkered cooking hot dogs over the fire. I didn't want to ask about the salmon, maybe they were saving it, but Teddi read my mind and smiled her calm smile. 'Hot dogs cook quickest!' she said.

Jeanette was listening to her iPod. I don't know what she was listening to, but I liked the way she travelled: with her iPod in one pocket, her traditional Yup'ik woman's knife, or *ulu*, in the other.

Something vital had broken in the engine. We were too many, strictly speaking, for one boat, so it was decided that Patrick would wait alone on this bank, with the defunct boat, the fire and the gun.

The rest of us would continue upriver for a while. We wouldn't reach the mountains, but we'd go see what we could see.

As we left Patrick sitting cross-legged by the fire, I asked him, 'Are you not scared?'

'Scared o' what?' he replied. He spoke with the modesty or reticence I'd come to admire in the people here, especially the young.

I shrugged. The size of the place. Loneliness. The cold, black clouds. Hungry bears.

'Done it before,' he said. 'All night.'

'Scared of what?' said his father. 'This is our backyard.'

I don't know how many miles we travelled, because the river looped so much. In time, however, the riverbanks grew into soft hillocks, and thicker bushes crowded the banks. Then, at a place where the river split in two channels, Warren nudged the boat ashore at the north bank and anchored it with a metal plate thrust into the earth. We left the boat and scrambled up a steep bluff covered in low vegetation, leaves already crisped with autumn hints. When we'd climbed about two hundred feet above the water we reached a rounded summit where bedrock was breaking through, and what I saw from there astonished me. I saw land. Every way one turned, the tundra was laid out like a green sea, sedgy and subtle and glinting with secret melt pools and waterways. It was land relishing its brief summer, open and free to breathe. To west, south and north the land seemed unbounded, but eastward, inland, there rose range after range of low, grey-blue mountains, the source of the river, with shadows in their glens and corries. Above all, the sky. Every hue of sky was present at once, here a shower, there rays of sunshine filtering through, there openings of blue, and every white and grey of cloud. The shadows of clouds drifted over the land. It was a dream vision, a mythic view of land before farms, before towns and roads, unparcelled, unprivatised, whole.

We sat on the ground in the light breeze. Warren lit a Marlboro, Jeanette offered more lollipops. I sucked a red one, and could have looked out over that land forever. In a sense, Warren and Teddi and Jeanette have been. I was aware of them beside me, and I wondered how their thoughts ran when they got out here, away from the village and the corporation and the US government and all the social problems and well-intentioned schemes, and just looked at their land, land they had managed to retain. I wanted to say, 'Please, enough of the Smith and Jones. Please tell me your Yup'ik names. Tell me what you're thinking, what you're looking at, when you get out here.' But I didn't. There was their reticence to consider, and I didn't want to annoy them with questions. On the other hand, I'd pass this way but once.

Warren was squatting a few feet away, his camouflage jacket hunched over his shoulders. After a few minutes I plucked up courage and said, 'Warren, this is some backyard.'

He smoked on silently, but then he seemed to relent. With his cigarette between his fingers he pointed southward over the intricate, mazy land, all sage green and emerald green and russet. He said, 'That's where I go wolf-hunting.'

Then he pointed east, over the plain spread before the mountains, and said, 'One time, 'bout five years ago, I came up here and all that place was covered in caribou . . .'

'How long have you people been here?'

'About ten thousand years. In winter we come up here on snow machines. Go over to Eek.'

Winter was when the river froze and snow fell and the difference between land and river and marsh was abolished. A time to socialise – if it snows. Last year, unusually, there had been none.

The others reappeared over the brow of the hill. They'd been off scouting for bears but had had no luck. Jenny wanted to see a bear because she was going home to Scotland soon, and there hasn't been a wild bear in Scotland for a thousand years. But there were no bears nearby, Teddi said, because there had been no snow last winter.

Apparently, no snow means few berries the following summer, and if there are no berries to eat, the bears won't stick around. 'They'll be at the salmon-spawning grounds on the side creeks,' she said.

Warren was still gazing over the tundra below. 'Our elders taught us to look for ravens. When a raven swoops, something is down there. If there's a bunch of them, they might be following a moose or a bear. If you suddenly hear seagulls, something's crossing the river.'

The land was so flat, and the air so clear, you could have seen a raven, or heard a gull, miles away.

Too soon we had to leave, edging back down into the confines of the river channel to the waiting boat. Down there, the dream vision of the land was gone.

Back at the shingle beach, Patrick had kept the fire burning. The rain had passed. Again the sisters set to work – now we would eat salmon. They took one of the morning's catch, wrapped it in tinfoil and set it in the hot embers. Then the fishing lines came out again, and as the first fish baked, they landed more. 'Subsistence fishing', they call this. Despite the grocery store, many villagers still live off the land. Winter would soon come, and supplies had to be laid down. When the salmon was ready we hunkered round the fire, eating its hot, pink flesh with our fingers, and it was good. Then came a gateau bought from the store, only slightly bashed. Having eaten, we travelled downstream again, bringing Patrick with us. They'd come back another day for the boat with the faulty engine. Right now we were going with the flow, still looking out for bears, for moose and beaver and birds, though the noise of the engine would most likely scare them away and it was mid-afternoon, bear siesta time.

But we weren't done fishing. Some miles down we put into a certain creek, a slow green backwater aside from the main river. Here, in the waters around a grassy islet, flashed the scarlet sides of sockeye salmon, dozens of them. Like silk slashes in a Tudor sleeve, the red fish parted the water's surface as they moved. Again we left the boat, again the rods came out. It was appalling. Having spawned, the salmon were rotting even before they died. Red and stylish in the water, they emerged from it like things of nightmare, mouldering, hook-faced, blotched. They were so plentiful all our hosts had to do was choose one, throw a hook at it and haul it in. One after another the fish were landed. They flapped listlessly on the mud, then were beaten over the head. Fifteen, then twenty fish skulls broke with a wet smacking sound.

As Teddi had predicted, bears had indeed been here, and perhaps still were, though we couldn't smell them. On the ground among the riverside shrubs were strewn the half-chewed bodies of a dozen fish. Such profligacy!

Having killed the fish, Teddi sliced off their heads with the curved blade of her *ulu*. The red flesh would be cut into strips, then hung to dry on wooden frames down at the village. When she threw the salmon heads back into the clear water, dozens of smaller fish shoaled round to investigate.

I wasn't going to get off without fishing, and soon enough Warren handed me his rod and line, and showed me how to hold it. I stood in the stern of the boat and inexpertly dangled the hook in the water. In two minutes a trout came, simple as that, like a magic creature out of a folk tale, surrendering itself to me. I pulled and wound it in, the rod bending, the fish's colours gleaming as it rose.

For the few weeks of the digging season, the archaeologists took up residence in the village hall, which served as refectory, social hub, Wi-Fi station and laboratory. Sometimes in the evening Quinhagak people came by to see what we'd been up to, and to examine the day's finds. They came in ones or twos. Mostly, they spoke little, but if we did have conversations I noticed how often and how modestly they described encounters with the natural world. For example, one evening after work Teddi came by. She sat next to me at a long plastic trestle table. I don't know how the subject came up, but in her soft voice, she told me about a cloud that had once come to her aid. She had been picking berries alone out on the tundra, and had stayed too long. She had become exhausted and a bit sunstroked. Then, out of a clear sky, right above her, a little cloud had formed itself. The cloud let down rain, filling leaves with water for her to drink. How grateful she was to that cloud! More than one person expressed the opinion that the tundra is watchful. They said, 'Out on the tundra, it's like something's looking at you.' Sometimes you see odd things there.

John Smith is an elder with a penchant for blue jeans and Johnny Cash, who carves artefacts from walrus ivory. He told me about an encounter he'd once had with a spirit woman 'just this high' who had appeared before him, dancing to the beat of her tiny drum.

Another man told me about hunting a bear. He spoke with no self-aggrandisement or swagger. On the contrary. He'd been young at the time and out hunting with his father. 'Shoot it!' his father had said. He'd shot the bear. His father had scored lines on the dead bear, as if he was going to skin it. Then the father handed the knife to his son, saying, 'Your bear, your responsibility.'

'It took me three days to skin that bear. I never hunted bear again.'

If you imagine all these incidents together, all the looking and listening, the stories and encounters, remembered and repeated and layered over thousands of years, built up slowly like the frozen peat of the tundra, you might indeed come to know your own backyard. And how it might help you. From two different sources I heard the story of the young man, some decades ago, who went with friends out onto the sea ice. They'd been hunting, but he somehow got separated from the others, and when he tried to reach land and home he couldn't, because the ice had drifted away from the shore. Alone on the ice, he survived *for four months*. All he had were the clothes on his back, and his tools and weapons – and the knowledge his elders had bequeathed him.

I was told these stories not in a sod hut, lit by a seal-oil lamp, certainly not in an igloo, but in the village hall – a metal-clad shed raised on stilts, harsh with electric strip lights. The hall was itself a disused grocery store, scheduled to become a bingo parlour. Does that matter? The stories came from people so softly spoken, and arrived so unexpectedly, and were over so soon, I wondered if I'd heard them at all. They were there and then gone. For a visitor like myself they offered a glimpse of a vastness, like the sight of the land we were afforded when we went upriver.

The next day Warren was again striding towards his office, harassed as ever, cell phone pressed to his ear, but when he spotted me he came over to deliver a formal thank-you.

'In our tradition,' he said, 'the first fish you catch you must give to an elder. I gave your trout to my mother. She sends her thanks. She says, "Now my belly is full." ' ■

Mouse Trails

I love the night filled with its dry awakenings
Like my X, filled with dust and cobwebs.
Friends, that's as lazy as it gets. The distorted
Railroad, the unsettling pre-depletion. Bucolic

Tides at the hospital, the murder that has already
Been tried. What I am equipped to do is different
Than what I have been called for. That's a
Statement that cannot be retracted. There. The

Blood around the desert – we call this 'sport'.
The pugilistic greetings in doorways, the grass
Underneath these snows, love holds its humid
Moments like a sailor who has never arrived.

The thick exile of this parabolic season, the
Way you used to talk to me, gone into mouse trails.

A groundbreaking collection of the best new voices from the new *Paris Review*

For six decades, *The Paris Review* has discovered the great voices in American literature, from Philip Roth to Adrienne Rich to David Foster Wallace. *The Unprofessionals* introduces the new vanguard—writers who know that what they do is more than a profession, who treat writing as an art. It is, in the words of Akhil Sharma, "the best possible introduction to the best literary magazine we have."

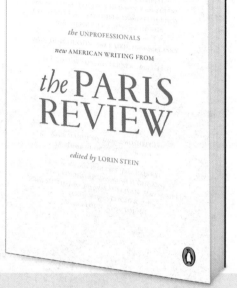

Including Emma Cline, Kristin Dombek, Ishion Hutchinson, Nick Laird, Ben Lerner, Ottessa Moshfegh, Benjamin Nugent, Zadie Smith, John Jeremiah Sullivan, and many more

"A new generation of writers is not only keeping American literature alive but restoring the excitement of it ... and *The Paris Review*, despite its age and pedigree, is at the forefront of the renaissance." **—JONATHAN FRANZEN**

"Good writers are always beginners, unprofessionals, driven by desire: ears open, vision wiped clean. They find their home in *The Paris Review*." **—HILARY MANTEL**

"This book is electric. I got to encounter voices I already loved and fall in love with writers I'd never read." **—LESLIE JAMISON**

On sale 11/17/15   Also available as an e-book   Penguin Books

The cross on the bank of the River Iza marking the place where Ianoş Paşca was murdered by Mărtin Grad, 21 May 2009.

THE HAND'S BREADTH MURDERS

Adam Nicolson

In the poor and remote province of Maramureş in the northern Carpathians, cut off by bad mountain roads from the rest of Romania to the south, the ancient body measures persist. Anything approaching six feet long – a plank of wood or a table – is a *râf*, the span of a man's arms; a *cot* is a cubit, from elbow to fingertip; a *ţol* – about an inch – is the length of the last joint of the thumb; and a *palmă* is a hand's breadth, the distance between the outstretched tips of the thumb and fingers of one hand.

Sitting in a cafe or in people's kitchens over a cup of coffee or a glass of *palincă*, the same *palmă* gesture recurs: the fingers held out over the table, tensed, overstretched, the most that a hand can cover. The *palmă* isn't much, but it isn't nothing, something you can imagine mattering more in a moment of passion or fear than it would before or after.

The word can turn metaphorical, so that a *palmă de pământ*, a hand's breadth of land, can stand for those little patches, the slim border zones between holdings, pieces of land whose ownership is uncertain, which are also sometimes called 'battlegrounds', *luptă terenuri*, literally 'fighting lands'. Every year in Maramureş neighbours kill each other for these contested slips of territory. At times in this mountain province there have been forty such violent attacks in twelve months, and week after week, much as road accidents are described in other parts of the world, the local press reports another man – always a man – *ucis pentru o palmă de pământ*: killed for a hand's breadth of land.

After the act, the murderers usually give themselves up, shocked at what they have done, going back into their kitchens to wait for the police to arrive and, when the case comes to trial, pleading guilty, as if something had burst up within them for which they were not responsible.

I have wondered if this is a glimpse into antiquity, beyond the agreements of modernity; an archetype of the failure of human relations, or at least an eruption of the underlying facts of rivalry, loathing, violence and hatred? It is certainly behaviour as old as any record of human life. In the *Iliad*, Homer compared the Greeks and Trojans fighting across a blood-spattered wall to 'two men, with measuring-rods in hand, tussling over the landmark stones in a common field', and Patrick Kavanagh, remembering an incident at home in Ireland in 1938, when the neighbours were suddenly at war over 'half a rood of rock, a no-man's land':

> heard the Duffeys shouting 'Damn your soul'
> And old McCabe stripped to the waist, seen
> Step the plot defying blue cast-steel –
> 'Here is the march along these iron stones.'

Kavanagh called his little fourteen-line poem, in which the rhymes never quite rhyme, 'Epic' because:

> Homer's ghost came whispering to my mind.
> He said: I made the *Iliad* from such
> A local row.

We – I – now live almost entirely insulated from these competitive realities. Our rivalries are expressed in remarks at home, after a party when the guests have gone, or in non-replies to emails or phone messages. In that way our relationships are made and unmade almost at will. Physical neighbourhood – the ever-present neighbour-touch of poor farming life – is not like that, and seems older and more elemental. In Maramureş it is, for example, the practice to bury large stones along your boundary, only parts of which appear at the surface. They are difficult to move and it would be even more difficult to conceal the marks of their having been moved, but they also work as a kind of psychic fact. Their dark and buried bulk, powerfully present in their hiddenness, known but unseen, have threat crouched within them, the silent but implicitly violent distinction between what is yours and what is mine.

This is an old practice but there is something slightly more complicated in play than the survival of ancient behaviour into modern life. The hand's breadth murders in modern Maramureş are something more disturbing than that, signs of modern dysfunction and dispossession, of traditional systems failing, of the modern substitutes proving inadequate, of naked, unregulated behaviour leaving in its wake decades of pain and grief, widowed women and orphaned children.

I was in Maramureş with the photographer Gus Palmer and Romanian journalist Teofil (or 'Teo') Ivanciuc. We went looking together for the stories behind these murders. The first piece of land we found for which a man had died was a *palmă* of 1,800 square metres, or 0.44 acres.

It is about fifteen yards wide and about one hundred yards deep, next to the long fast road that runs through the village of Săcălăşeni in north-western Maramureş. The village is now a dormitory suburb for the provincial capital Baia Mare just to the north, with fewer than thirty cows where even ten years ago there used to be seven hundred. An air of lifelessness hangs over it, with no one about in the daytime. On the patch of murder-land, which has been uncared for since the killing, you have to push through a thick pelt of buttercups and foxtail grasses to reach the willows that are now springing up along the boundary fences.

Just along the road, the dead man's brother, Ciprian Radu, is living in a small house at the side of an unused yard – no animals, no muck. This is the house where his brother was killed three years ago. It is a weekday mid-morning. Ciprian is welcoming but he has been drinking and his handsome, high-cheekboned face is flushed and puffy. There is a smell of drink in the air and both maleness and poverty seep from the walls. A soft-porn calendar hangs in one corner of the living room, a tapestry of da Vinci's *The Last Supper* is up behind the sofa, there is a crumpled paper icon of Christ pinned by the door and, on the television, people in traditional Maramureş costumes perform songs for a bare-shouldered hostess while colours flicker on the set.

In April 2012 the three Radus – Ciprian, his elder brother Calin, a big man aged thirty-five, and their younger brother Petru, twenty-eight, anxious and flighty – were here in their grandmother's house. It was a holiday, one week after Easter, in the middle of the day and they were drinking: *palincă*, the plum brandy which features in most of these stories. Calin, over eighteen stone, had just been left by his wife. He was unhappy as she had kept the children. Petru was getting overwrought. 'He had a nervous disease,' Ciprian says. And so Calin rang for an ambulance to take him to hospital. 'But Petru could be aggressive when he was drunk.'

An argument started about the land. Calin had been working for many years in England, as a builder and in a car park. He had also had some money from their mother. Petru suggested they sell the land down the road – it had belonged to their father – but insisted that the proceeds should be shared only between him and Ciprian. Calin surely had enough money already. 'I was trying to separate them,' Ciprian says, 'but I couldn't stop them arguing so I left.' It was a familiar situation: they had been arguing for years and Ciprian was away from the house for about forty minutes, to visit his aunt, but more than anything to escape a scene he hated.

When he was away, Petru, who was only eight or nine stone, took a knife that happened to be lying on the table, simply to threaten and scare Calin. 'He just touched him with the knife on the right shoulder, not a deep one. He had no plan to kill him but he just touched the artery and the blood started to flow. Just there.' Ciprian pointed to the corner by the door, the brown carpet below the paper Christ.

Ciprian is anxious with the memory. 'When I came back, the knife was outside, covered in blood. Calin was lying down here on the bench still alive. The room was bloody and he was pale and bloody. Petru was lying on the other bed here.'

By the time the police and ambulance arrived Calin was dead. 'I thought when I went away the fight was just with fists, but when I came back I saw the knife and I understood what had happened. How easy it is for someone to die. It was almost an accident. How easily someone can die. A little stab and someone dies. It was that, a little stab.'

Ciprian seemed still to be suffering a form of shock. Something was inexplicably missing, the dead brother removed from life as if by a force that had arrived momentarily in this house, leaving him pale and gasping on the bench, and then killing him.

Petru tried to plead in court that he had acted in self-defence, that Calin had come for him, but there were no witnesses and the magistrate did not accept the plea. The crime was thought particularly severe because it was brother murdering brother, a breaking of bonds within the family. Petru was sentenced to pay one hundred euros a month (about a quarter of an average monthly wage) to the dead man's little daughters, and the judge recommended that Calin's widow should have the equivalent of €20,000 from the murderer. She refused to ask for it 'because she understood it was an accident. And knew that Petru did not have this money.' Or so Ciprian says. Petru is in Gherla Prison now, a place for serious criminals, sentenced to ten years, as severe as any hand's breadth murder sentence because, as Ciprian says, 'They were brothers. The accidental nature of the crime was not taken into account.' He will probably be out in five years. Calin's widow now lives in England. And the family goes on as if catastrophe were part of the weave of life.

E very piece of land is important here. People in Maramureş, with an inheritance of poverty and crowdedness, are what they are because of the land they have. Land is a constituent of the person. To enter another man's land, particularly the yard around his house, is as intimate a penetration as putting your fingers in his mouth. A sophisticated, multilingual journalist in Baia Mare, who did not want to be named, told me that if someone came 'into his land' – that was his expression, as if the land were an entirely enclosed space – he would kill him. 'It is a border he has crossed. And when he sees my eyes he would understand. It has happened to me, men coming onto the land with guns. I told them they had to leave within ten seconds. "If you enter again, I don't give you the chance." '

One evening in the main street of Săliştea de Sus, a big raw-boned village in the valley of the River Iza, we talked to an old lady called Ileana Vlad. She was sitting and knitting on one of the 'gossip benches' that line the street outside every farm gate. Things were not going well, she said quietly.

'My husband died on the fifteenth of December. Now I cannot find a little pig in the market. And you can't live without a pig and some chickens. It's only women left now. All the men are in the cemetery. A life without a man is not worth living. Why not? Because there is no one left to do the repairs! What can we do?'

She was knitting a black winter waistcoat with sparkly red and green threads in the wool. I asked her about land murders in the village. Not pausing from her needles, she said, 'Oh yes, a man killed a shepherd two years ago up there' – she pointed to the meadows on the valley side high above us, below the forest edge, where the cherries were in blossom and the beech trees were coming into new leaf. 'He killed him with a fence post; he shoved it into his mouth' – she gesticulated – 'because the shepherd walked over his land with his sheep. One eye of the shepherd jumped out onto the ground when the stick went in. He was from Moldavia.' This unlikely phenomenon appears in the *Iliad* too, when Patroclus smashes a stone into the forehead of a Trojan prince Cebriones 'and both his eyes jumped out into the dust at his feet'.

Ileana's lack of surprise, the click of her needles, her acceptance of extreme violence as part of how things are, the making of the winter waistcoat in the warmth of the spring sunshine, the need for a pig – all of it is part of a phlegmatic attitude to life, a lack of fuss at how difficult existence can be.

In the outdoor ethnographic museum in Sighetu Marmaţiei – a project of the passionately nationalistic Ceauşescu years – where the most beautiful examples of Maramureş wooden architecture were gathered before they disappeared from the villages, there is one house from Vadu Izei, a few miles up the road from Săliştea de Sus. It had belonged in the late nineteenth century to the two Arba brothers. When their parents died, they could not agree on how to divide their inheritance. Rather than kill each other, they decided, in effect, to kill the house and together sawed it in half. One half remained in the old farmyard with one brother while the other took his timbers and rebuilt his half in another part of the village. Only in 1970 did the museum in Sighetu buy both halves where they are now reconnected as a single house.

Walk through any of these valleys in the springtime and nothing is more impressive than this all-embracing physicality – the intimate connection of body with place and mind, the ways in which the physical elements of existence are dense with social and emotional meaning. One morning early last May, Gus, Teo and I were walking along the lanes of a little side valley above the River Iza, near the big village of Ieud. It was the moment at the end of winter when the land has to be 'arranged', as they say; cleaned and cleared for the growing year. People – mostly the old; not the young men and women away earning euros – were out on the roads. Farms are tiny – half of all the nine million farms in the EU are in Romania – and made up of even tinier strips scattered across the parishes. Almost no one has a car and so this is a walking world. No motor noise, no jet sound. Cuckoos and woodpeckers in the woods, skylarks above us, cocks crowing in the farmyards. The whole valley was filled with people ploughing, hoeing, axing out the dead wood, levelling molehills, cutting bean sticks, planting potatoes, raking old leaves, putting out dung. Women walked at the heads of the horses, the men behind at the wooden ploughs. Pastures were being scoured with ox-drawn dredges, ploughlands broken up with horse-drawn harrows. The last cartloads of hay were being taken back to the winter barns before the cattle were let out onto the spring grazing. The only sound on the road was the oiled creak of the cart axles as they passed.

It is easy enough to feel bewitched by the charm of this landscape, of people living in an animated, Bruegelian, pre-mechanised world, as if the experiences of Coleridge in Germany in 1799 or of Goethe in the Roman Campagna were still available to us now. The whole of Maramureş is like the Arba house in the Sighetu Museum: if you didn't know better, you might think it perfect – that no damage had ever been done. But then, in another light, you see the tools of violence being carried into the fields: the steel crowbar, the *ranga*, for making holes in the earth, the axe with its bright and burnished edge, the cleft oak posts, the hoes, the hedge slashers – all the instruments with which control and management can be imposed. Cutting, controlling, slicing, hacking, killing: these are aspects of everyday existence.

Vasile and Ioana Sas were walking along the road, an axe and hazel-handled rake in his hand, a checked work bag and hoe in hers. They were off to arrange some of their land. She walked on but Vasile stayed to talk.

He has twenty pieces of land and walks to all of them 'because I like walking!' He grows potatoes and beans and hay for his two cows. As we talked you could hear people having conversations half a mile away on the far side of the valley and the crackle of their fires as they burned the dead branches that the winter snows had brought down. Some of Vasile's pieces of land are miles away. How far? I asked. 'Oh, over there.' He pointed to a horizon where the snow was still lying in the forest. 'The other side of that, twelve miles from the village, each way.'

L and matters in Maramureş and ownership is a form of emotion here. A cluster of Romanian terms, all with the root *mos*, emerge in words meaning 'giving birth', 'inheritance' and 'land'. Land is memory and family, a form of manhood and womanhood, a way of being in the world, a mooring and fixity, a tangible identity beyond the fluidities and threats of life. 'Without land I always felt anxious,' one Transylvanian farmer told the anthropologist Katherine Verdery. Earth is flesh here.

Both geography and climate reinforce the idea of defensiveness as the core relationship to land. Maramureş is almost entirely mountain, high, hard and forested. Wolves and bears still live here. The only valuable land, from which bread can actually be derived, is down in the narrow valleys, where people cluster, where villages are almost continuous ribbons of buildings along the valley roads, and the strips of land are as treasured as any family heirloom. 'We are Maramureş,' Teo said only half ironically. 'We are very aggressive, very nervous. Everyone here will always reach for the knife in his pocket.'

The ethnic mix of the country also plays its part. A large majority is Romanian but scattered in among them are villages of Hungarians, Germans, Ukrainians, Gypsies and even Armenians. Your own land has its boundaries, but your language community is limited too. Even within the Romanian valleys, every village tells contemptuous stories of every other: the people of Bogdan Vodă have no forest left because they burned all their wood in the distant past, trying to boil a boulder which they thought was the egg of a dinosaur; the inhabitants of Săliştea de Sus are 'bumblebees' because a half-deaf old lady once heard the noise of a bee trying to get out of a window, thought the Tatars were coming to kill and rape them all, rushed to ring the bells of the church and the whole village ran away into the mountains and the woods; those in the very poor village of Strâmtura are called 'the ones who put the bull on the church roof' because in a drought they ran out of grass but decided they had to save the village bull. The men of the village hauled the bull up on the roof of the church, but by the time they got it up there it had died from the strain.

This is high and late country. The growing season was always thought to be one hundred days at best (that has lengthened with global warming), limited by frosts in May at one end and heavy rains in September at the other. Life had to be squeezed out of that growing year and most families were unable to survive without the wages earned by men labouring elsewhere in Romania and Austro-Hungary. 'People here have always been fighting for their life,' Dr József Béres of the Sighetu Museum says. 'The land is mine, it is my family's, it came from the past. The word peasant might mean "a man in love with the land", but there is not enough land. Big land was always occupied by the nobility and so the peasants were always short of it. It is a form of devotion but also of unending anxiety and desperation, a predicament shared with every neighbour you have.'

In 1848, the Transylvanian serfs were liberated and a large land-owning peasantry developed. From the 1860s onwards, each fragmented, multi-strip holding was carefully mapped and described in a meticulous Austro-Hungarian cadastral system. There were many local ways of policing this complex pattern of land ownership. Villages employed field wardens, *gornici*, to mediate in arguments between neighbours: where the boundaries lay, where cattle could or could not graze, whose hay grew in which meadow. The *gornici* were organised by a *birau*, a 'mayor of the fields', paid by the village, either through a local tax or by receiving the fines raised from malefactors.

But little was stable here. After the defeat of Austro-Hungary in the First World War, 3.9 million hectares were distributed to Romanian peasants; in 1945 a further 1.4 million hectares were expropriated from the German peasants and one million hectares redistributed. Communism and the collectivisation of most farmland in the decade after 1949 was only the most radical link in this necklace of disruptions. Along with the local authority of the priest, the council of elders in each village was done away with. Most land and all tools were gathered up, even the yokes of the cows, the ploughs, the wheelbarrows. The agents of the party, the New Men, usually the landless, the poorest in the village, became the agents of confiscation. People talking of that time can become speechless with the pain of it. The richest and most influential villagers, who employed others or had wide networks of cousins and supporters, were given impossible quotas or tasks – to plough, for example, their entire ten-hectare holding in one day – and could be imprisoned if they failed.

The New Men began to impose collective solutions and in the 1950s violent neighbour-hatred ballooned. Administrative change can scarcely address the loyalties of the heart and, needless to say, ancient memories of possession and belonging persisted under the new collectivised regimes. Those ghost memories of ownership – with the pain of dispossession rising up into the surface of everyday life – lie behind the murder of a farmer called Todor Lumei in the autumn of 1972.

His daughter Viorica, now fifty-seven, lives next door to her sister Maria, five years younger, in the house they were both born in. It is on the western edge of Sighetu Marmaţiei, tucked up in a little valley, the whole of which once belonged to their family, above the River Tisza. From their land they can look out over the gantries and towers of the salt mine at Solotvyno across the border in Ukraine and to the dark, cloudy forests beyond it. The sisters have divided the small wooden house in two and each has raised a family in their own inherited half. Cherry and apple trees blossom around their yards and gardens where the onions are already set. Dogs are kept in wooden runs, swallows sit on the telephone wires and chickens peck among the fallen blossom petals on the grass.

The worn air of loss fills Viorica's hot yellow kitchen. She tells the story, twisting her hands, folding and unfolding her fingers, while Maria listens, playing with the buttons on her phone.

'We were poor because our father died very early,' Viorica says.

'The whole hill here was once owned by our grandfather. But during Communism many others were settled here. The road is still our property but . . .' A shrug and half a smile.

'I was fifteen in 1972. It was in the autumn. And I was grazing the sheep with my younger brother. He was fourteen. We were looking after the lambs in the field up here' – she points to the hill behind the house – 'and the lambs went off into another piece of land, part of the collective farm then, and they ate some hay from the collective farm haystack.'

Next to that haystack was the little wooden house and yard of the man who had made the hay for the collective. It was not his hay, but he had done the work and built the stack. 'His wife started to shout and scream at us from her yard. "What are you doing? Your lambs are eating our hay!" '

Just then, by chance, her father came up the hill. He heard the woman shouting at his children. 'So he said to her, "Why are you making that noise? Why are you arguing with the children? If you have something to say, say it to me. I am here." He went into their farmyard to deal with it. "If I did something against you, just tell me, we can sort it out." '

Then the neighbour's small dog tried to bite Viorica's father. All his attention was given to keeping it away. And while he was concentrating on the little dog, the woman came up behind him and stabbed him with a little knife in the back. 'He was not deadly wounded,' Viorica says. 'It was just a small wound. He didn't pay attention to it, because he was still fighting the dog. Then the woman shouted, "Come and kill him! If you don't come and kill him, I will kill you!" Her husband came out of the house with an enormous knife and stabbed my father with it in the back and he fell down dead in one second.' With her hands she measures out the length of the blade on the plastic of the tablecloth, about two feet apart, each hand slightly cupped.

Viorica shouted for her brother and when he got to her and saw what had happened, they both started to scream so loudly that they could be heard in the town of Sighetu. Her brother ran down the hill to call for help. The murderer ran down after him, trying to stab him too, but he escaped. Then, quite suddenly, the murderer came to his senses and went into his house, with his wife, to wait for the police. Viorica stayed in the farmyard by the body of her father on the stones and the muck from the animals.

The neighbour was arrested. At court his family arranged things so that the wife was not accused and the murderer was sentenced to eight years, so little because he was already sixty-eight. During Communism, many general amnesties were issued and after one year and two months he was released. 'For such a murder,' Viorica says, half under her breath.

Compensation was set by the court. The neighbour was employed by the collective farm and sold his animals to pay the lawyers, so there was nothing left to give the children in compensation for their father's life. The murderer had no goods, so they received only his small wooden house: 'Seven by four metres, a room and a porch.' It was valued at 17,000 lei, fifteen monthly wages at that time, but that figure draws sceptical laughs from the women. 'It was worth much less but we took it,' Maria says. 'It was rotten, very rotten and so we didn't have much timber from it. We built a barn with it.' The man's wife died when he was in prison and afterwards he moved away. 'And can you believe,' Viorica asks, 'he lived until he was over ninety?'

What explains this? Why the rage of the murderer's wife? There had been no trouble before. But the ghosts of history were in play. The murder site had never been part of Maria and Viorica's grandfather's property, but memories of class distinctions hung on. They had been rich peasants; the murderer was the poorest of the poor. The land on which the haystack stood and on which he had made the hay had been his before collectivisation. And so rage and resentment and the grief of loss found its outlet in this. Had their father somehow, even inadvertently, been acting the richer peasant? Had the murderer's wife thought he was coming for a fight, and so attacked him first?

These questions drift around the kitchen, as they have these last forty years. After the murder Viorica went to work in a restaurant and then a hospital to help her family. She has been sick ever since. 'I was so deeply affected that I have had several strokes. Of course you can never get away from it. It is always in your mind. It is always in my memory.' Their mother fell sick. The family borrowed money from relations for the funeral and to cover the fees of the priests, working for years to pay them off. Grief took up residence beside them.

We went up the hill to see where the killing had happened. The meadow has been planted since then with a new plum orchard, the trunks painted white, the trees coming into leaf, the blossom already falling like spring snow onto the grass. A neighbour saw us walking up there. 'Look,' Viorica shouted. 'We have found some boyfriends so we are going out into the woods!' But it was no weather for picnics.

The revolution of 1989 released a surging demand for restitution of the lands that had been collectivised during the years of Communism. Over 1.5 million Romanian farmers started court cases against their neighbours for land claims in the 1990s. Those who had been using the land during Communism thought they had as good a claim to it as the descendants of those who had owned it before. Many of the descendants had moved away and were now in the cities. How did they have more of a right to land than those who had been working it for decades? Corruption and complexity swamped the process. Village land commissions, run by the mayors and deputy mayors, became the means of rewarding friends and punishing rivals. Land which had been built on entered an ambivalent state: who did it belong to, the original owners or the owners of the houses? It was decided in the 1991 legislation that those who once owned the land on which others had built now lost the right to one thousand square metres of it – the area occupied by a house and a small garden – but could claim the rest of it, plus an equivalent of the one thousand square metres in another part of the village. But this meant that land had to be invented.

People had forgotten where their land was meant to be. The cadastral maps, which were ignored by the Communists and recorded nothing that had happened since 1948, were rejected in favour of hazy witness statements. As Verdery has described:

> Fields have drifted from their original moorings in space. Even reference to the roads or ditches was not certain, for these too had changed in the meantime.

Earlier she had written:

> Whole fields seemed to stretch and shrink; a rigid surface was becoming pliable, more like a canvas. It was as if the earth heaved and sank, expanding and diminishing . . . How can bits of the earth's surface migrate, expand, disappear, shrink and otherwise behave as anything but firmly fixed in place?

Verdery has said that decollectivisation 'became a war between competing social memories' – between those who thought a pre-Communist system was restorable and those who treasured their own immediate pasts in places they had come to think of as home. It was a war fought, she says, 'on shifting sands, for the surface was now wholly relativised.'

By mid-1994, 6,236,507 claims had been filed for the return of land. 4,897,573 were accepted, for a total of 9.2 million hectares, two thirds of Romania's farmland. Just less than half of all holdings were under one hectare, 82 per cent under five hectares. But fog still hangs over the whole process. It remains unclear whether there are twenty-three million or forty-five million separately owned parcels of land in Romania. Poverty governed the territory; the price and number of horses both rose in 1990s Romania as few could afford any other form of farm equipment. What now looks like traditional peasant agriculture is in many cases not the persistence of ancient patterns but a symptom of the collapse of what had been a relatively advanced form of collective agriculture. In some ways, Romanian farmers were demodernised in the 1990s.

In this last great twentieth-century dissolution of the known order, hand's breadth murders peaked again and on into the new century, just as they had in the 1950s.

It is Saturday and Marisca Orha, the seventy-five-year-old widow of Ioan Orha, is in the kitchen of her house in Tămăşeşti, a village out in the rich, open country in the west of Maramureş. Her daughter Rodica, who lives in Baia Mare where she runs a tyre business with her husband, is visiting her mother as she usually does at weekends. Together they are brushing up the feathers on the earth floor from the chicken they have just plucked. Its naked body is lying on the table, with a stump where the head once was. A pot of something is stewing on the stove.

'He wasn't guilty,' Marisca says when we ask about her husband. There is another hen and thirteen little chicks in a small enclosure by the stove, and while Marisca talks, the hen clucks quietly over them and they cheep in reply. 'He died for nothing. The piece of land, it is just along there. You can go and look at it if you like. Go later. Have some wine. Nobody enters my house without receiving something.' She brings a plastic bottle of her delicious fruity wine, the smell of grapes still in it, and Rodica fetches a big hank of paprika-stained lard which we eat in little rectangles with bread and peppers. Her kitchen is filled with an enveloping warmth.

Her husband's great-grandfather had taken care of the land during the war. Originally it was 1.5 hectares, although now it is only a third of that, 4,600 square metres, just over an acre. At the time, under the fascist Hungarian regime then governing Transylvania, he had also taken care of the Jews who owned it. Until May 1944, there were about 40,000 Jews in Maramureş working in the villages as farmers, shepherds and foresters. Some five thousand of them survived Auschwitz, and after the war the Jewish family that owned the land gave it to Orha to thank him for the trouble he had taken over them. 'All officially done,' Marisca says, with a rising urgency in her voice. 'All with papers.'

During collectivisation the Communists took the land and made parcels of it, distributing it to different families to use. 'And after the revolution each farmer moved back to his old field that was previously his own. But with this piece of land – it is called Ograda Jiga from the Jews who had it before – one family said that it was theirs. They had been working it for as long as anyone could remember. Even though Ioan had all the papers proving his right of ownership.'

The other family was called Sabou, and in 1997 the case went to trial in Baia Mare. 'Father was very busy with his work here,' Rodica says, 'and so he did not go to the trial.'

'We had no money to pay a lawyer,' Marisca says. 'We thought if we had the papers it was enough and we didn't need a lawyer.'

'But he lost because he was not there. We made an appeal but we lost that too and so we abandoned the field.'

Nobody used it for fifteen years. The land lay neglected, a weed-filled strip, 'unarranged', between pieces of land that the Orhas farmed carefully, planting them with maize. In March 2012 a young man from Baia Mare called Marinel Daniel Sabou, the thirty-year-old nephew of the Sabou who had won the case, needed it to graze some sheep he had just bought. 'Sabou came here to see the boundary with his friend Petru Pocol. They came into the courtyard to ask Ioan to show him exactly where the field boundaries were, just to check they weren't trespassing on another man's field. So he went with them.

'When he arrived back he was bleeding. He said, "I am dying." He said that here at this door. "I was heavily beaten by them." '

Why?

'Because when they arrived at the land, they said, "Let's measure it with our feet." "No," he said, "bring a tape. Doing it with your feet is not good enough. You can get it wrong so easily with your feet." '

Now, with the memory, Marisca begins to shout in her kitchen. 'They were so angry. They kicked him *here*' – she put her hands to her ribs and stomach – 'until they broke his organs inside. He came back in such a bad state, so we called the ambulance and police.'

Why did they do it?

'They were just angry and they turned to violence.'

'It was a Saturday,' Rodica said, 'and the police told my mother: "We don't come out for such a small case." '

'He was lying there on the bed then,' Marisca went on. 'They said: "You, Marisca, you must come to the police station on Monday to report it." '

An hour later the ambulance came but while she was waiting Marisca took a hay fork and went herself to the field and found the two men there.

'Your husband was lucky,' they said to her. 'He was not young enough. If he had been young enough to fight we were going to kill him, but we decided not, so we just left him lying there because he was so old.'

She pushed the hay fork at them. ' "You bitch," they said to me. "You thief." '

His spleen, the doctors said, was not broken. It was 'exploded'. He lost 2.5 litres of blood to internal bleeding. They operated on him as soon as he arrived in hospital, but they could not do much, and after five days in intensive care he died.

Two weeks after the funeral one of the Sabou cousins came up to Rodica in the street in Baia Mare and proposed to make peace. 'It is a shame that such a young man should go to prison and your father was old and not far from dying anyway.' She told him that she had nothing to say and justice must follow its course.

The next time the Orhas saw the young men who had killed their father and husband was at the trial. As Marisca caught sight of them she had a heart attack. Since then, she has had two strokes. 'The worst part for me is that he died for nothing. He wasn't guilty and for that I suffer, still today.'

The men were both given eight years in prison, of which they will probably serve four, contemptible sentences which are the surest sign that the process was corrupt. Even today the land is empty. No one goes on it. Rodica took us there in the light spring rain, smoking with the anxieties of memory. 'They never came back to graze it. It is all for nothing. My mother is suffering a lot but she is a fighter. She never stops.'

Goldcrests chirred in the hazel clumps beside us. Did Rodica have any photographs of her father? 'No. I have taken them all to Baia Mare. It is not good for her to see him now.'

Back in the house, Marisca looks up at me, a golden tooth in her smile, her flowery, black-and-white apron like something a girl would wear, her black scarf on her head. 'They came in March, that heavy day, just to measure the border. "Come with us," they said. And so he went.'

Can one see any of this from the other side? Is it really possible to regard murder, as the laughable sentences handed out to the killers imply, as a normal part of everyday life? Of how things are? Of what men do to each other – as unfortunate spontaneous eruptions of anger which do not need to disrupt the flow of life? Could I see how these land murders looked from the point of view not of the victim's family but the killer's?

There had been one particularly horrible murder on the edge of Săliştea de Sus, where the victim, Ianoş Paşca – a big, violent and angry ex-miner from a family of famous anti-Communist partisans – ended up lying dead in the shallows of the River Iza. The local press had been able to photograph him one long afternoon in May 2009, his shirt up over his hips and the back of his head bloody.

He had been sitting on the riverbank across from his house, just at the spot where a favourite cousin of his had been killed years before, accidentally electrocuted when illegally electrofishing in the river. Paşca had bought the land a few years previously – good valley land but only 1,800 square metres, or just less than half an acre, a *palmă de pământ*, something and nothing – because it was ancestral ground. His grandfather used it but his father had actually bought it and then given it as a dowry for one of Paşca's sisters. Paşca then 'paid good money for it' – 30 million old lei or about €750 – to his sister. His wife, Ileana, had urged him not to buy it because, as she said to me, 'Everyone wanted it. It was fighting land. There were many other things he could have bought but he bought that land. His mind was fixed.'

The person who wanted it more than anyone was Paşca's cousin Mărtin Grad, a small man, known as Mărtinuc or Little Martin, who lived in the same village. His father and Paşca's were brothers, and Mărtinuc and all the Grads thought that in some way, despite the documents to the contrary, the slip of land, just at the point where the side valley called Tătarului comes down to the Iza, should belong to them. Paşca and Mărtinuc had been at each other's throats for years. Paşca had complained more than twenty times to the police that Mărtinuc was threatening him. And he had said to Ileana, 'I am going to kill him.' She had said, 'Don't touch him. You only have to hit him and he will die.'

The *palmă de pământ* is a sweet spot: the green sward in May is covered in dandelions and daisies. Pear trees run along the public road, loaded and thickened with blossom. Willows have been pollarded on the riverbank itself, and there is a woodyard to one side, tangy with newly cut oak.

On 21 May 2009, the feast day of saints Constantine and Helen, Mărtinuc had been drinking with a friend. It was a holiday and just before four o'clock in the afternoon he stood up and told his friends, 'Now I am going to kill someone.' Paşca was sitting on the river-bank with Mimi, his treasured three-year-old granddaughter, in his arms. Mărtinuc crept up behind him and hit him in the back of the head – it is generally thought with an axe, or perhaps with a split-oak fence post. He tried to kill Mimi too, to get rid of a witness, but he was drunk and she ran away. She remembers her bag dropping into the river.

Mărtinuc went home, said, 'I killed him,' and waited for the police. He was given twelve years, will serve six and is due out this year.

Paşca's widow Ileana was awarded 100 million old lei compensation for murder, about €2,300, but she has yet to receive it. Worse than that, when she came home from court and walked past the gate to the killing land, Mărtinuc's family, quite illegally, were there with their hoes and forks. As she walked past, one of them said: 'We will kill you just as our father killed your husband.'

Ileana Paşca lives in a state of dread. She is sixty-seven and has spoiled her eyes 'with cheap Russian glasses'. Her face is saggy with emotion and exhaustion. Mimi, her granddaughter, spends much of her time with her, solemn and almost entirely silent, perhaps permanently traumatised by the scene she witnessed six years ago. Meanwhile, gossip ripples around the village: that Mărtinuc had been looking after the chief of police's sheep; his children had been making the chief of police's hay. Mărtinuc himself had been in the front row of church every week and the priest loved him. Ileana told me that the priest had even visited him in prison and urged her to forgive him. To which she shot back, 'If your wife had been killed, would you be ready to forgive the murderer?'

I started asking in the village for Mărtinuc's family. It wasn't easy. Mărtinuc? Mărtin Grad? Aren't there two people of that name? The one who killed that man by the river and walked off? Oh no, I don't know that one. I know the other one. Then going on their way down the village street, the relief palpable in their bodies, the cigarette in one hand, the small black hat resettled on the top of the head. Or, with people who were connected to him, that look of difficulty and defence, of thoughts in mind that are not to be expressed, an inwardness, a retraction below the surface of the face, even while stirring the coffee or working the till. No, not a nice person. It isn't enough to go to church. He wasn't a good Christian. Perhaps even a false Christian you could say. Not an honest man. And that result was final proof, wasn't it? People had entertained their suspicions before.

A man drinking coffee in the Irimi cafe bar, Dan Iuga (he had lost his right index finger to an axe: 'No problem! One less fingernail to clean!'), thought there might be a relation – Mărtinuc's daughter's mother-in-law – living just along the street, but it turned out she was away in hospital in Cluj. Ioana Iuga, running the bar and related both to the Grads and to the Paşcas, thought maybe Mărtinuc had some relations living up the little narrow valley called Tătarului, up in the hills, the very valley at the foot of which he had clubbed Paşca in the head.

A stony lane curls its way up the valley alongside the stream, with willows and cherries in blossom the length of it. Here and there are tiny poor farms. The wild and its threat are not far away. It is called the Tatar Valley, a name which suggests that, as an impoverished valley on the very edge of things, it was somewhere for the poor, marginalised sub-groups of the Tatars, not good enough for Romanians. Over the poultry runs, single, tattered chicken wings hang from willow sprigs to keep the hawks away.

Little strips of meadow are slipped into the foot of the valley. Most of the ground is too steep to plough or dig, so steep, one farmer told us as we passed, that the upper plough horse would always be tumbling down over the other if you tried. The forest is a solid wall above the lowest few yards of the valley, full of oaks and new beeches, their leaves alight with spring green. High cherry trees were blazing like lanterns among them. Thrushes and blackbirds sang in the shadows. Pied wagtails dipped and bobbed on the river stones. It is bear and wolf country. Three years ago, one winter night, 150 sheep and eight dogs were killed by a pack of three wolves about fifteen miles from here, outside Rona de Jos. Teo was carrying a pepper spray in his pocket, more for the dogs than anything else. 'I have been bitten too often in places like this.'

We asked at the little houses for Mărtinuc's family. 'Yes, further up' – that waving, flicking hand gesture meaning 'not here, up there, further away'.

Finally we came to the place where they said Mărtinuc's daughter lived. Three dogs on chains guarded it from any approach. Each dog had worn to dust the ground within the reach of its chain. A tiny cabin, scarcely a house, stood a yard or two inside the fence and gate, with a ragged broken henhouse and pig house beside it. A haystack stood in the yard and chickens picked around the straw. There was no spot of level ground. Five yards from the door of the house, the wall of the valley rose into the forest. Washing hung on a line attached to a cherry tree.

It was a beautiful corner but no one would live here unless they had to. And thinking of those lovely level square metres of land by the river, where a family could spread itself in ease, and with the knowledge that whatever they planted would grow in the alluvium on which they lived, you might well feel that envy and hatred was inseparable from being stuck up here in the beauty of this hard and impoverished place.

We stood at the gate and a middle-aged woman came out of the house, short-sleeved shirt, strong arms, an unquestionable presence about her, and we began talking. She was Ioana Grad, Mărtinuc's daughter, married to Ioan Vlad who was away this afternoon working on the railway. Her son-in-law was on the far side of the yard, clipping the wool from an old ewe, with his wife and baby daughter beside him. He saw us, stood up and slowly walked over, the pair of long-bladed cutters in his hand, held out in front of him, the blade upright, his fist around the handle resting on his thigh, his eyes under a peaked forage cap intently fixed on us as we stood there outside the yard, talking to the woman across the gate, not crossing the all-important boundary. The last words of this family to Ileana Paşca were in my mind. There is no mistaking the big, swinging, self-establishing manner of a fighting man and we reacted as animals do in these circumstances, looking down and away, no meeting of those eyes, no encounter with the cloud of defensive, frightened aggression he was emitting, nor with the cutting blades held out in front of his thigh.

We talked about the EU, how no grants were available for farmers with less than fifty sheep, or farms as tiny as theirs; about the valley, their goats, the weather and the bears. 'Is that why you are here?' Ioana asked. 'Because Ioan was bitten by the bear?' 'Ah yes,' I said, 'because of that.' And with this talk the air of threat and distance started to shrink away. The son-in-law Stefan lowered his blade and Ioana asked us into the house. She had just baked an apple cake. Would we have coffee?

We sat beneath a small Day-Glo icon of the Holy Family at a table two feet square, covered in a plastic lace cloth. There were geraniums in pots growing in the window. They had tried to grow medicinal herbs here, but the plants had never thrived. They had made thirty carts of hay on the high meadows last summer and brought them down on sleds over the snow in the winter. They felt they had nowhere to go, nowhere to be. Unlike other, richer families from these valleys, they don't have the resources to go west within the EU to earn the sort of wages that can buy cars, build new houses and change lives. 'But you want to know about Ioan and the bear?'

It was 1991, the fourteenth of September, the Day of the Holy Cross. At ten in the morning, Ioan Vlad was looking after the cows only a few yards from the farm on the edge of the forest when a bear ran out between them. After Ioan hit it with a stick the bear put a thumb into Ioan's mouth and grasped his face with his other claws. 'With that one hand the bear broke all the bones in Ioan's face. He did not pull his face out but he broke it all,' his wife said.

Ioan, as they were fighting, with a presence of mind it is difficult to imagine, put two of his own fingers in the bear's nostrils so that it couldn't breathe. The bear dropped him and ran away. Ioan was screaming with pain and the neighbours came running from farther up and down the valley. His head was soon swollen to the size of a melon and they carried him down to the village, past the Paşcas' house to a place beyond the river where there was a telephone and an ambulance that could take him to hospital. 'All his body was torn because the bear had played with him. In Cluj, he had seventy-two operations on his face and still now he cannot eat easily because some of the bones in his head are still loose. And one of his eyes can no longer have any tears.'

Is that why they have so many dogs chained up around the edge of their place? 'Well, for Gypsy thieves, for foxes, for wolves, for hawks. You never know. For bears. For strangers. For our enemies.' Then looking out of the open door, to the lane and the stream and the steep far wall of the valley, filling the space of the doorway, no more than twenty yards away, 'Do you know how much I like to talk like this?'

Ioan returned from work, one half of his face visibly slumped and broken. 'Everything you see on my face was down,' he said. 'You could see the other side of this eye. And this is the eye from which tears will not come now.'

While Stefan and his wife Maria returned to clipping the urine-coloured wool from the old sheep, Ioan took me to see his cow and as he talked he held her lip tenderly and sweetly between the fingers of his hand. 'She is a lovely creature, isn't she?' he said.

Such gentleness and such intimacy in a world where violence seems as natural as the blossom on a springtime tree. If Homer made the *Iliad* from such a row, he also knew that there is no boundary between violence and love, that the two coexist in the same hand, the same face, the same slip of contested territory. It is not that these valleys are particularly violent places; only that in such a deeply corrupt society, with government ministers and officials siphoning off subsidies meant for farmers, dodgy bank deals, the abuse of power by local bigwigs, magistrates, the police and even the postmen, all living in a culture of mutual scavenging, taking whatever their power will allow them to take, violence is the resort of the dispossessed. That is true whether it is the bear threatened in his diminishing forest or the poor marginal farmers for whom flat and fertile land at the foot of the valley looks like a paradise of riches. Was it so inconceivable, in this place high up in the valley of Tătarului, that you might attack and kill another man you hated because he owned something which you thought was yours? Would you not feel justified in killing him because his ownership of that land itself felt like a kind of murder? It is a logic of claim and revenge that Achilles would have understood. It is what happens in a place where revenge is the only justice. ∎

THE HAND'S
BREADTH MURDERS

PHOTOGRAPHS FROM MARAMUREŞ

Gus Palmer

A *palmă* is a hand's breadth, the distance between the outstretched tips of the thumb and fingers of one hand. A *palmă de pământ*, a hand's breadth of land, can stand for narrow pieces of land whose ownership is uncertain.

Minutely divided strips of farmland outside Breb, Maramureș.

Ciprian Radu, brother of Calin Radu. Calin was murdered in the village of Săcălăşeni in 2012.

In the Radu house, in Săcălăşeni, north-western Maramureş.

Ileana Paşca, widow of Ianoş Paşca, who was killed in Săliştea de Sus on 21 May 2009.

Ileana Paşca holds the deed to the land over which her husband Ianoş was killed.

Site of the murder of Todor Lumei, killed here in the autumn of 1972.

Viorica and Maria Lumei, daughters of Todor Lumei, at home.

Marisca Orha in her kitchen in Tămăşeşti.

Pig fat prepared with paprika by the Orhas.

Ioana Grad, daughter of the murderer Mărtinuc Grad, at home in Tătarului.

Pig shed in Tătarului.

Ioan Vlad, son-in-law of Mărtinuc Grad. Vlad's face was clawed by a bear in 1991.

Ioan Vlad pinches the lip of his beloved cow.

Same magazine, different format

New app out now

GRANTA.COM

GRANTA

THE MAGAZINE OF NEW WRITING

PRINT SUBSCRIPTION REPLY FORM FOR US, CANADA
AND LATIN AMERICA (includes digital and app access).
For digital-only subscriptions (includes app access), please visit granta.com/subscriptions.

GUARANTEE: If I am ever dissatisfied with my *Granta* subscription, I will simply notify you, and you will send me a complete refund or credit my credit card, as applicable, for all un-mailed issues.

YOUR DETAILS

TITLE ....

NAME ....

ADDRESS ....

....

CITY .... STATE ....

ZIP CODE .... COUNTRY ....

EMAIL ....

☐ Please check this box if you do not wish to receive special offers from *Granta*

☐ Please check this box if you do not wish to receive offers from organisations selected by *Granta*

PAYMENT DETAILS

1 year subscription: ☐ US: $48   ☐ Canada: $56   ☐ Latin America: $68

3 year subscription: ☐ US: $120   ☐ Canada: $144   ☐ Latin America: $180

Enclosed is my check for $ _____ made payable to *Granta*.

Please charge my: ☐ Visa   ☐ MasterCard   ☐ Amex

Card No. ☐☐☐☐☐☐☐☐☐☐☐☐☐☐☐☐

Expiration date ☐☐ / ☐☐

Security Code ☐☐☐☐

SIGNATURE .... DATE ....

Please mail this order form with your payment instructions to:

Granta Publications
PO Box 359
Congers, NY 10920-0359

Or call 845-267-3031
Or visit GRANTA.COM/SUBSCRIPTIONS for details

Source code: BUS132PM

ALMEIDA
THEATRE

Winter 2015/16 Season
NOW ON SALE

19 November 2015 – 9 January 2016

LITTLE
EYOLF

**by Henrik Ibsen
adapted and directed by Richard Eyre
from a literal translation by
Karin and Anne Bamborough**

5 February 2016 – 26 March 2016

UNCLE
VANYA

**by Anton Chekhov
a new version created by Robert Icke**

almeida.co.uk
Tickets **020 7359 4404**

Supported using public funding by
**ARTS COUNCIL
ENGLAND**

Principal Partner

ASPEN

THE MIDDLE AGES: APPROACHING THE QUESTION OF A TERMINAL DATE

David Szalay

1

It is light when he leaves the hotel. Light. Primordial sunlight disclosing empty streets, disclosing form with shadow, the stucco facades. And silence. Here in the middle of London, silence. Not quite silence, of course. Never true silence here. The sublimated rumble of a plane. The burble of pigeons courting on a cornice. A taxi's busy rattle along Sussex Gardens, past the terraced hotel fronts, from one of which he now emerges.

He feels that he is leaving London unseen, slipping out while everyone else is still asleep, as he walks, with his single small holdall, to the square where he left the car. The square is hotel-fringed, shabby. A few benches and plants in the middle. Sticky pavements. The car is still there, surrounded by empty parking spaces. It is not his. He is simply delivering it. Slinging his holdall onto the passenger seat, he takes his place at the wheel, on the plump leather.

He sits there, enjoying the feeling of inviolable solitude. Solitude, freedom. They seem like nearly the same thing as he sits there.

Then he starts the engine, which sounds loud in the silence of the square.

He is aware now that he does not know exactly which way to go.

He looked yesterday and it all seemed simple enough, the way out of London, south-east, towards Dover. Now even finding his way to the river seems problematic. He tries to picture it, the streets he will need to take. When he has formed some sort of mental picture of where he is going, and only then, he pulls out.

He waits at a light on Park Lane, some posh hotel on one side, the park on the other, staring sleepily straight ahead.

When he gets to the river there might be a problem. He hopes there will be signs for Dover. The possibility of getting lost makes him mildly nervous, even though he would not be in any serious danger of missing the ferry. He has plenty of time. It is his habit, when travelling, always to allow more time than he needs.

He went to sleep very early last night. The previous night, Friday, he had been out late, with Macintyre, the Germanic philology specialist at UCL. And then he had had to get up early on Saturday to take the train to Nottingham and pick up the car from its previous 'keeper', a Pakistani doctor. (Dr N. Khan was the name on the documents.) He had done the whole thing on a hangover, which had made the day pass over him like a dream – made it seem even now like something he had dreamed, the time he spent in Dr Khan's front room, looking through the service history, while the doctor's cat watched him.

He swings around Hyde Park Corner, the sun pouring down Piccadilly like something out of Turner, the palaces opposite the park half dissolving in a flood of light.

He squints, tries to push it away with his hand.

Macintyre had not been very helpful. He was supposed to have looked at the manuscript, the section on Dutch and German analogues in particular. They had talked about it for a while, in The Lowlander. Macintyre, with a suggestion of subtle mockery that was entirely typical of him, always insisted on meeting there. The early modern shifts in German pronunciation, for instance. The way some dialects ...

He has to focus, as he flows through them, on the layout of the streets around Victoria Station.

The way some dialects were still impervious to those shifts, after more than five hundred years.

The traffic system pulls him one way, then another, past empty office towers. He looks for the lane that will throw him left eventually, onto Vauxhall Bridge Road.

There.

No, Macintyre had not been as helpful as he might have been. Obviously, he was holding back. Professional jealousies were evident. He did not want to give too much away about what he was working on. That was why he had wanted to talk about other things. Kept steering the talk away from shop. Wanted to know, when he had had a few Duvels, about his 'sex life'. 'How's your sex life, then?' he had said.

Well, he had mentioned Waleria. Said something about her. Something non-committal.

The lights halfway down Vauxhall Bridge Road start to turn as he approaches them and after a moment's hesitation he stops.

Macintyre was married, wasn't he? Kids.

The lights go green. Unhurriedly he moves off. A minute later – the Thames. That exhilarating momentary sense of space. The water, sun-white.

Then streets again.

In south London he feels even freer. These are streets he does not know, that may be why. Strange to him, these sleeping estates. These hulks, slowly mouldering. He has a vague idea that he needs to find the Old Kent Road. Old Kent Road. That insane game of Monopoly that happened in the SCR once. He thinks of that for a moment, and imagines the Old Kent Road to be liveried in a drab brown.

Signs for Dover draw him deeper into the maze of south-east London. The maze marvellously unpeopled – the low high streets with their tattered shops. The sun shines on their grubby brick faces. Dirty windows hung with curtains. Only at the petrol stations are there signs of life. Someone filling up.

Someone walking away.

He has so much time, he thinks he might make the earlier ferry. His own 'sails', as they still say, just after eight. So yes, he may well make the previous one – it is not yet five thirty and already he is in the vicinity of Blackheath, already he is merging onto an empty motorway, its surface shining like water. Speed. There is a tangle of motorways here. He must keep an eye out for signs.

Yes, Macintyre has several kids. No wonder he seemed so threadbare and fed up. So tetchy. Some little house somewhere in Outer London, full of stuff. Full of noise. He and his wife at each other's throats. Too worn out to fuck. Who wants it?

CANTERBURY says the sign.

And he thinks, with a little frisson of excitement, *This is the way Chaucer's pilgrims went. Trotting horses. Stories. Muddy lanes. And when it started to rain – a hood. Wet hands.*

His dry hands hold the leather-trimmed wheel. Through sunglasses he eyes the wide oncoming lanes. He has the motorway to himself.

Wonderful to imagine it though. The whole appeal of medieval studies – the languages, the literature, the history, the art and architecture – to immerse oneself in that world. That other world. Safely other. Other in almost every way, except that it was *here*. Look at those fields on either side of the motorway. Those low hills. It was here. *They* were here, as we are here now. And this too shall pass. We don't actually believe that though, do we? We are unable to believe that our own world *will* pass. So it will go on forever? No. It will turn into something else. Slowly – too slowly to be perceived by the people living in it. Which is already happening, is always happening. We just can't see it. Like sound changes, spoken language.

'Some Remarks on the Representation of Spoken Dialect in "The Reeve's Tale".'

The kick-ass title of his first published work. Published in *Medium Ævum* LXXIV. Originally written for Hamer's *Festschrift* – Hamer who had supervised his doctoral work when he first turned up at Oxford. A tall, bald man with spacious, elegant rooms in Christ

Church. Would literally offer you a sherry when you arrived – *that* old school, that English.

The author of works such as: *Old English Sound Changes for Beginners* (1967). Professor Hamer lived, it had seemed, in a fortress of abstrusity. Asleep at night, he must have dreamed, so his young foreign pupil had thought, sipping his sherry, of palatal diphthongisation, of loss of *h* and compensatory lengthening.

And he had envied him those harmless dreams. Something so profoundly peaceful about them.

Something so profoundly peaceful about them.

Everything so settled, you see. It all happened a thousand years ago. And the medievalist sits in his study, in a shaft of sunlight, lost in a reverie of life on the far side of that immense lapse of time. The whole exercise is, in its way, a memento mori. A meditation on the effacing nature of time.

He likes the little world of the university. Some people, he knows, hate it. They long for London.

He likes it. The fairy-tale topography of the town. A make-believe world of walled gardens. The quietness of summer. The stone-floored lodge and the deferential porter. Yes, a make-believe world, like something imagined by a shy child.

Somewhere to hide.

Dreaming spires.

Sun sparkles on wide motorway.

It is just after six and he will be at Dover, he estimates, in an hour.

Yes, he likes the little world of the university. He *likes* its claustral narrowness. Sometimes he wishes it were narrower still. That the world of the present was even more absent. He would have quite enjoyed, he thinks, the way of life of a medieval monastery – as a scholarly brother, largely exempt from manual labour. He would have enjoyed that.

With, naturally, the one obvious proviso.

Without noticing, he has pushed the car well into the nineties. It manages the speed without effort. He eases off the accelerator and the needle immediately starts to sink and for the first time this morning he feels sleepy – a mesmeric sleepiness induced by the level hum of the engine and the monotonous, empty perspective in front of him. It seems, for long moments, like something on a screen, something spewing from a CPU. Just graphics. Without consequences. He shakes his head, moves his hands on the wheel.

Yes. The one obvious proviso.

Last year, during the Hilary term, he had done the thing he had long wanted to, and had an affair with an undergraduate. It had been something he had had in view since his arrival in Oxford to finish his doctorate. It had taken years to achieve – and the affair itself, when it finally happened, was in many ways unsatisfactory. Just two weeks it had lasted. And yet the memories of it, of her youth . . .

He was sad in an abstracted way, for a day or two, when she ended it with that letter in her schoolgirl's handwriting, that letter which so pathetically overestimated his own emotional engagement in the situation. And he understood that he had also overestimated her emotional engagement in it. As he had been intent on enacting his own long-standing fantasy, so she had been enacting a fantasy of her own, in no way less selfish. Except that she was nineteen or twenty, and still entitled to selfishness – not having learned yet, perhaps, how easily and lastingly people are hurt – and he was more than ten years older and ought to have understood that by now.

Only when he saw her, soon after, in the arms of someone her own age – some kid – did he experience anything like a moment's actual pain, something Nabokovian and poisonous, seeing them there in the spring sunlight of the quad.

And by then he was already mixed up with Erica, the medieval Latin scholar from Oriel. That didn't last long either. It lasted one summer.

The days he has just spent in London have exhausted him. Not only the meeting with Macintyre. He also had a meeting with his publisher. And a symposium on Old English sound changes at UCL, for which he was one of the speakers. Various social things.

He had seen Emmanuele, the short, snobbish, scholarly Italian who had finished his DPhil a few years before and was now a lawyer in London. Emmanuele had asked after Waleria, what was happening there? It was at a party at Mani's, last September, that he had met her. 'I don't know,' he had said. 'Something. Maybe. We're seeing each other. I don't know.'

Solitude, freedom. There is that feeling, still, on the ferry. This in spite of the other people; they are transient strangers, they do not fix him in place. They know nothing about him. He has no obligations to them. Sea wind disperses summer's heat on the open deck, hung with lifeboats. The floor see-saws. Is sucked down, then pushes at his feet. England dwindles. The wind booms, pulls his hair. Inside, in the sealed warmth, people eat and shop. He wanders among them, nameless and invisible. Sits at a table on his own. His solitude, for the hour it takes to travel to France, is inviolable. He stands at a window, golden with salt in the sunlight. He watches the playful waves. He feels as free as the gulls hanging on the wind. Solitude, freedom.

As soon as he has driven off the ship he puts on the A/C and Vivaldi's 'Gloria' – pours into the French motorway system with that ecstatic music filling his ears.

Dum-dee

Dum-dum-dum-dee

Dum-dum-dum

The asphalt glitters. It is Sunday morning. Farms lie in the flat bright land on either side of the motorway.

And he knows this motorway well. It follows the so-called Côte d'Opale, towards Ostende. To the left as he drives are the windy dunes.

WELKOM IN WEST-VLAANDEREN says the sign.

And now it is like he is driving through his own past, through a landscape full of living nerves, of names that are almost painfully evocative. Koksijde, where he once went with Delphine and her mother's dog – the small dog digging in the sand among tufts of wind-flattened grass. Nieuwpoort – where they spent that summer, he and his parents. The smell of the sea finding its way inland, up little streets – and at the end of the streets, when you walked down them to meet the sea with your plastic spade in your hand, a milky horizon. Roeselare, where they would visit his father's parents – the suburban house, with hop fields at the end of the neat garden. Though the memories possess a jewel-like sharpness they seem surprisingly small and far away, as if seen through the wrong end of a telescope. It has been years since he was here, on this flat tract of land next to the ship-strewn sea, and that his own life has been going on long enough now for things like that windy day at Koksijde with the little dog to lie more than ten, more than fifteen years in the past is somehow a shock to him. He was already an adult then, more or less, and yet he still thinks of his adulthood as something that is just getting under way.

Feeling a little shaken, he stops for petrol.

Holding the nozzle in the tank he stares at the motorway, the thin Sunday traffic.

That desire for everything to just stay the same. That day at Koksijde stretched out over a whole lifetime. Why is the idea of that so appealing? Or today, this very moment, the hum of the flowing petrol, its heady sickening smell. The motorway, the thin Sunday traffic. Here and now. The pallid heaven of these hours. Solitude and freedom. Stretched out over a whole lifetime. That desire for everything to just stay the same.

The tank is full.

Walking back from the till – where it felt strange, somehow, to speak his own language with the woman there – he finds himself enjoying the sight of the luxury SUV in which he is travelling. The paintwork is a kind of very pale caramel, with a hard metallic shine. The windows are just perceptibly tinted. He feels pleased and proud to take his place in it, to start the engine with the touch of a button. Stańko is trusting him to hand it over, to sign the papers that will transfer the ownership. And though he does not know him very well

– has only met him once, in fact – Stańko has every reason to think that he *will* hand it over.

Stańko is, after all, a policeman. The senior policeman of Skawina, a town in southern Poland, nowadays a suburb of Kraków – tractors farting in fields of potatoes next to a multiplex showing the latest films.

You don't fuck with Stańko. Not in Skawina or the neighbouring townships, in Libertów, or Wołowice.

It is easy to picture him in this pale caramel car, moving through the banal landscape of his beat, his wallet abulge.

How that brooding ogre and his ugly little wife produced something as lovely as Waleria . . .

Well, maybe she wouldn't age well. It was worth thinking about, though he feels no inclination to long-term thoughts. He still doesn't see things that way. It still feels new, this situation, even somehow provisional. There was a sense, for some time, that they had no obligation to each other, that they were free to see other people. He didn't. (Unless you include Erica the Latinist, who was still, last September, just about extant.) Whether Waleria did or not he doesn't know.

He has turned inland, passed Bruges.

Later, Ghent, where he did his undergraduate degree. English and German. *Sir Gawain and the Green Knight. Parzival.*

After Christmas he spent a few days in her parents' Day-Glo orange house. A scalloped balcony over the white front door. Snow disfiguring all the garden ornaments. Waleria met him at Kraków airport and drove him to the house, which was near a petrol station on the edge of Skawina. Hills nudged into the sky, somewhere in the distance.

Every day while he was there he and Waleria went skiing at Zakopane. ('Do you ski?' she had asked him, making small talk, when they had first met, at Mani's party. 'Do I ski? I'm Belgian,' he had deadpanned. It made her smile.) She was an excellent skier, in her powder-blue jacket, her fluffy white hat. Warily, he had followed her down the stiffest slopes Zakopane had to offer.

As he approaches Brussels, clouds close over him in the sky.

Wind moves the trees at the side of the motorway. There will be rain. Shafts of hard light pick out the distant prominences of the city as he passes. He knows the way without having to think about it – the leaky underpasses, the glimpse of Uccle (those tree-lined avenues, where he was once a bookish schoolboy who lived in a big flat), and then out on the E40 towards Liège, as the rain starts to fall. He feels for the lever that sets the wipers swinging.

Since then, since Christmas, they have seen each other every few weeks. A sense evolved that they were in some way together, a sense of mutual obligation. He wouldn't put it more strongly than that. Sometimes she visits him in Oxford, or they spend a weekend in London, or somewhere else. They meet, for the most part, in the neutral spaces of hotels. There was Florence in February. There was, at Easter, a week in the Dodecanese, island-hopping, the windy deck of the hydrofoil in its world of vivid blues.

Slowly, they are finding each other out. 'You,' she said, 'are a typical only child.'

'Which means?'

'Selfish,' she told him. 'Spoiled. It never occurs to you,' she said, 'that you might not be the centre of the universe. Which is what gives you this personal magnetism you have . . .'

'Now you're flattering me . . .'

'It's nerdy,' she said. 'Still, it's there.'

She was shuffling her cards, her tarot pack. That was a surprise. It seemed she had this New Agey side to her – it wasn't, he told himself, fundamental to who she was.

'OK. You're going to take three cards,' she said. 'Past, present, future.'

They were lying on his bed. Oxford. It was Saturday morning. Last month.

'So.' She offered him the pack, fanning it out. 'Take one.'

Humouring her, he prised out a card.

'Ace of Wands,' she said. 'Past. Take another.'

'The Tower.' She made a face of mock alarm. 'Fuck. Present. Last one,' she instructed him. And said, when he had taken it and turned it over, 'The Emperor. Future.'

'That sounds good,' he suggested, looking pleased with himself.

She was studying the three cards, now lined up crookedly on the sheet. 'OK,' she said, provisionally. 'I *think* I understand.'

'Tell me.'

'It's time to grow up. That's the headline.'

He laughed. 'What does *that* mean?'

'Well look at this.' She was pointing to the Ace of Wands. She said, 'It's obviously, you know . . . it's a phallic symbol.'

It did seem to be. The picture was of a hand holding a long wand, which thickened towards the top into a fleshy knob, a divided hemisphere.

'Yes,' he said. 'So it seems.'

'Well that's the *past.*'

'What – so I might as well kill myself now?'

'Don't be silly.' It was difficult to say how seriously she took this. She looked quite solemn. 'The present,' she said. 'The Tower. Some kind of unexpected crisis. Everything turned upside down.'

'I'm not aware of anything like that.'

'That's the point. You won't be, until it hits you.'

'Unless it's you.'

She ignored that. 'Now let's look at the future. The Emperor – worldly power . . .'

And he made some silly remark about how that sounded like him and started to fondle her nipple, to tease it into life. They were naked.

She said, 'I think these cards are suggesting that you should maybe stop thinking about your . . . *thing* all the time.'

He laughed. 'My thing?'

'This.'

She put her finger on it.

'What it means,' she said, looking him in the eye, 'is that your skirt-chasing days are over.'

'But I don't chase skirt. I'm not that type.'

'Oh yes you are.'

'I promise you,' he told her, 'I'm not.'

It is ideal, he thinks, the set-up they have. He is unable to imagine anything more perfect. He is unable to imagine living more happily in the present.

The huge sheds of the Stella Artois plant at Leuven, its steaming stacks, are half obscured by the drenching weather.

How well he knows this stretch of motorway, its different surfaces, the sound of the tyres shifting suddenly, dropping in pitch, as you pass from Flanders to Wallonia. How often, in the years he was studying in Ghent, did he drive it, and how insignificant a distance it seems now, as part of his longer journey – he is already halfway to Liège and it feels like he has only just left Brussels.

And now here it is, Liège – the place where the road plunges down into the valley, the dirty old city suddenly spread out, exposing its memories to the low grey sky.

Pines start to appear in the woods that margin the road as he mounts the heights on the other side of the valley, overtaking trucks in the slow lane.

Suddenly fresh, everything.

Not soiled by mouldering industry and memories of youthful pain like the grey town in the valley.

He needs to finish the piece for the *Journal of English and Germanic Philology*; he was hoping to have it done by now. The question of whether, in the pre-West Saxon period, *æ* sometimes reverted to *a* – or whether in fact the initial change from *a* to *æ*, postulated for the West Germanic period, that is to say prior to the Anglo-Saxon settlement of Britain, never in fact took place at all. The principle evidence for the former hypothesis was always the form '*slēan*' – if *that* form could be shown to be anomalous, then the whole venerable thesis would start to look very questionable. Hence the importance of his proposed paper, already accepted in principle by the journal, 'Anomalous Factors in the Form "Slēan" – Some Suggestions'.

He had used some of the material, teasingly, in his talk to the UCL symposium last week. Quite a stir. (The look on Macintyre's face!) Yes, this might be it – the thing he has been looking for, the thing that makes him, in the world of Germanic philology, a household name. Something everyone in the field simply *has* to have read. Worldly power. So he must take time over it – seclude himself with it for the rest of the summer. Stop thinking about his *thing* all the time.

He is eating a chorizo sandwich, drinking Spa water.

Sitting in a huge Shell services with a Formula One theme. Francorchamps is nearby, somewhere in these forests.

There are not many people about. Even though it is high summer – the second week of July – the weather is foul, and there is little to do up here in the woods when the rain is just steadily falling, seeming to hang whitely against the dark slopes of pines.

With cold hands, he puts more petrol in the car. He has an idea that it is cheaper here than in Germany. He isn't sure. Stańko is paying for the petrol anyway. He tucks the receipt into his wallet with the others as he walks out again into the rain.

This is where he leaves the road he knows – the motorway running east towards Cologne. He looks, sitting in the car while the rain falls, at the printed Google Map. An indistinct line drops diagonally down from where he is into Germany, just missing Luxembourg. The E42. It ought to be easy. He folds the map and sits there, in the rain-pelted car, finishing his coffee. Luxembourg. Never been there. Like Surrey was a country. Silly. *Anomalous.* Like '*slēan*'. A household name. He just needs to devote himself to his work. Stop thinking about his thing. Time to grow up. That's the headline. He had liked the way she said that.

The windscreen is a mass of trickles. Summer. Still, there is something romantic about the rain. There are not many people about. It was her idea to meet at Frankfurt airport. Not *the* Frankfurt airport – Frankfurt-Hahn, a no-frills-type place deep in the countryside, and nowhere near Frankfurt; Frankfurt doesn't even appear on his Google Map, even though the little pin indicating the airport is almost in the middle of it. They are used to airports like that. Sleepy places next to a village with twenty flights a day at most. They have been in and out of them a dozen times so far this year. In and out. In and out. It was her idea to meet there and finish the journey to Skawina together, taking their time, spending a night or two on the road.

2

The airport is harder to find than he thought it would be. There is more driving, when he leaves the straightforwardness of the E42, on narrow twisting lanes, more following tractors. A hilly landscape. The day is grey and humid. There is insufficient signage. He passes through a village, starting to worry that he might be late after all, and then quite suddenly it is there. He is soon moving among parked vehicles, looking for a space, in a hurry now.

He finds a space.

And then it happens.

There is a loud ugly metallic noise that for a moment he does not understand.

Then he does and his heart stops.

When it starts again he is sweating heavily.

She looks up from her magazine, smiles.

'Sorry I'm late,' he says.

'You're not late. The plane was early.'

'Everything was OK?'

She is putting her magazine in her bag. 'Yes. Fine. You must be tired,' she says, looking up at him. He appears pale and shaken. 'You've had a long drive.'

'I'm OK, actually,' he says. 'Probably it will hit me later.'

'Do you want something to eat?'

'Uh.' He thinks about it. He was hungry, half an hour ago. He has had nothing to eat all day except a pain au chocolat on the ferry and that chorizo sandwich, up in the rainy Ardennes. Now, however, he isn't hungry. In fact he feels slightly sick on account of what has happened to Stańko's luxury SUV. 'Maybe I should,' he says. 'Have *you* eaten?'

'I had something.'

'Maybe I should,' he says again.

'OK. Are you OK?' she asks, suddenly sounding worried.

'Yes. Yes,' he says. 'Fine.'

They speak English to each other. His English is more or less native-speaker standard. Hers is only slightly less perfect.

He queues at some sort of food place, one of only a few in the airport. The airport is shabby and unexciting. Modest improvement works are taking place behind plastic sheets and warning signs. He orders, in flawless German, a ham sandwich, a double latte.

'Look,' he says, sitting down next to her. 'There's something I need to tell you.'

To his surprise, her face instantly tightens. She looks frightened. 'Yes?' she says.

'I had an accident,' he says, taking the plastic lid off his latte. 'With the car. In the car park. Here. There's some damage. To the paintwork.'

She doesn't say anything.

'I hope your father won't be too pissed off.'

'I don't know,' she says.

'Do you want any of this?' he asks, offering her the sandwich. 'I'm not really hungry.' When she shakes her head, he says, 'How was the flight? OK?'

'Yes, it was fine.'

'From Katowice?' he asks.

'Yes.'

'We're staying tonight in a place called Trennfeld,' he says, soldiering on with the sandwich. 'It's a couple of hours' drive from here. According to Google Maps anyway.'

'OK.'

'Gasthaus Sonne,' he says.

Though she smiles at him, something seems to be wrong.

'OK?' he says.

She smiles at him again, and he wonders if it's just him – is he just imagining it, or does she seem nervous about something?

'Let's go?' she says.

He takes her little suitcase and they leave and walk to the parking, where she inspects, without passion, the huge scuff on the side of her father's new car.

He sighs, theatrically.

'See?'

'M-hm.'

'I hope your father won't be too pissed off,' he says again.

It starts to rain as he walks to the machine by the chain-link fence and pushes euros into it to pay for his stay.

When he comes back, she is sitting in the passenger seat, staring straight ahead.

There is some trouble about getting back to the E42 towards Frankfurt. They spend some time lost in dung-strewn lanes, the dull farm country.

When they are finally on the motorway, they travel at first in silence, as though hypnotised by the movement of the wipers, which are struggling to keep up with a downpour.

He is still thinking about the damage.

About how easily it might *not* have happened. If he had only arrived a few minutes earlier or later, for instance, he would surely have found a different place to park. There was one slightly tricky space near the entrance that he had almost taken – then he kept on looking, though the space he ended up in, after a few minutes of irritable prowling, was even tighter.

He had needed a piss. That might also have played its part – the way it made him still more impatient and unfocused on what he was doing. And he was tired and hungry and in a hurry and had been stuck behind a tractor for ten minutes while he tried to find the airport. And all of these things, all of these individually unlikely or indecisive factors had united in the fateful moment, had placed him exactly *then* and *there*, and the damage was done.

And what will happen about it?

He will have to pay for the fucking . . .

'There's something I need to tell *you*, Karel,' she says.

He doesn't quite understand the emphasis, has forgotten that he used the same phrase himself, half an hour earlier, in the airport.

'What?'

A long silence.

He is still thinking about how much the paint job will be, and whether Stańko knows someone who can do it for less than the usual price, when he notices that the silence is still going on.

'There's something I need to tell you,' she had said.

And the number of things she might have to tell him shrinks, as the silence extends, until there are only one or two left.

One part of his mind takes that in; the other part is still energetically fretting over the scraped wing.

She is either about to end their little affair, their succession of tousled hotel rooms, or

'You're pregnant,' he says, throwing the indicator lever, moving out to overtake in a tunnel of spray.

He hopes that she will immediately negative this.

Instead the silence just prolongs further.

Outside a wet, grey world unfurls around them, wind-whacked trees huddling at its edges, pouring into peripheral vision.

Part of him is still doggedly preoccupied with the prang. That is starting to drift away though, as if into infinite space.

'Are you?' he asks.

Those moments when everything changes. How many in a life? Not more than a few.

Here, now, the moment. On this rainswept German motorway. Here and now.

'That's shit,' he says, still searching the road ahead with agitated eyes.

Finally she had spoken. 'I think so,' she said. And then, 'Yes.'

'That's shit,' he says again.

The prang is far off now, though he is still just about aware of it, like some object far out in the darkness.

His whole life seems to be out there, divested.

What is left? What is he to wrap himself in, now that everything has floated off into space?

It hangs out there, in the darkness, like debris.

She is, he notices, shaking with sobs.

It takes him by surprise.

And then she starts, still sobbing, to hit her own forehead with a small white-knuckled fist.

'Stop it,' he says, glancing helplessly at her from the relentless, rain-curtained autobahn. 'Please,' he says. 'Stop that.'

'Let me out, stop the car,' she says through tears.

And then screams at him, 'STOP THE CAR!'

'Why?' His voice is shrill and frightened. 'Why? I can't . . . What the fuck are you doing?'

She had started to open the passenger door. Wind noise roared at her. Cold air and water were sucked momentarily into the civilised leather interior.

'Are you fucking crazy?'

Her tears redouble and she says, piteously now, 'Stop the car, stop the car . . .'

He stares more frazzledly at the oncoming world. Suddenly it seems unrecognisable. 'Why?' he says. 'Why?'

She has started to hit her forehead again, her fist knocking on the taut pale skin with a sound that inordinately upsets him.

And then an Aral station's lit pylon looms out of the rain – the blue word ARAL high above everything – and, indicating, he slows into the lake of the exit lane.

As soon as the car stops moving, or even a moment before, she is out of it.

He sees her, through the still-working wipers, walk away, hugging herself, and wonders, numbly, what to do.

He had just stopped on the apron of tarmac short of the petrol station. Now he lifts his foot from the brake and the car moves on at walking pace, under the huge canopy that protects the pumps from the rain.

He has lost sight of her.

One of the parking spaces in front of the shop is empty and he slides straight into it. With his thumb he shoves the button that kills the engine and then just sits there for a few minutes. That is, for a fairly long time. The life of the service station swirls around him, as if in time-lapse. He is staring at the stitching of the steering wheel, the elegant leather. There is a temptation just to drive away – drive back to his own life, which feels as if it is somewhere else.

There is no question of actually doing that, however.

Instead he discovers he has tears in his eyes.

Tears just sort of sitting there.

Tears of shock.

Inside the shop, he peers about, looking for her. He hangs around outside the ladies for a minute or two, as if she might emerge. He tries her phone.

He starts to worry that she might have done something silly. That she might have taken a lift from a stranger or something.

He is in the car again, moving slowly through the acres of parked trucks along the side of the motorway, when he finds her. She is still walking. Walking with purpose. She must have been walking all this time.

'What are you doing?' he shouts through the open window, keeping pace with her.

She ignores him.

He overtakes her and pulls into a space among the trucks some way ahead. He sits there for a few seconds, fighting a furious urge to just drive away. Instead, getting out of the car and hunching his shoulders against the rain, he takes his umbrella from the back seat. It bangs into place above him, and immediately fills with sound.

As soon as she notices it – it is very large and has 'University of Oxford' written on it – she turns and starts to walk the other way.

Only for show – he is able, with no more than a slight quickening of his pace, to draw level with her, and take hold of her arm.

A truck lumbers past and he drags her out of the way of its spray, into the puddled alley formed by two other stationary trucks.

'What are you doing?' he says. 'Where the fuck are you going?'

Her face is twisted into an unfamiliar tear-drenched ugliness.

This whole situation, this awful scene among the trucks, has taken him totally by surprise.

He waits for her to say something.

Finally she says, 'I don't know. Anywhere. Away from you.'

'Why?' he asks. 'Why?'

It has been his assumption, from the first moment, that there will be an abortion, that that is what she wants as well.

Now he starts to see, as if it is something still far away, that that may not be so. It is initially just something that his mind, working through every possible permutation in its machine-like effort to understand, throws up as a potential explanation for what she is doing. She does not want to have an abortion. She is not willing to have an abortion.

In a sense this is the true moment of shock.

He fights off a splurge of panic.

She has not said anything, is still just sobbing in the noisy tent of the umbrella.

He asks, trying to sound loving or sympathetic or something, 'What do *you* want to do?'

'You can't make me have an abortion,' she says.

He wonders, Is she a Catholic? A proper Catholic? She is Polish after all. They have never talked about it.

'I don't want to make you do anything,' he says.

'Yes you do. You want me to have an abortion.'

This he does not deny. It is not, after all, the same thing.

He says, again, 'What do you want?'

And then when she says nothing, he says, 'It's true. I don't think you should keep . . . Fuck, *stop!*'

She had tried to pull away from him, to leave the shelter of the umbrella. He is holding her arm now, tightly, and saying to her, '*Think* about it! Think about what it would mean. It might fuck up your whole life . . .'

She shouts into his face – 'You already have fucked up my whole life.'

'What?'

'You have fucked up my whole life,' she says.

'How?'

He asks again, '*How?*'

'By saying that.'

'What?'

'What you said.'

'What did I say?'

'That's shit,' she says.

His face is a mad mask of incomprehension.

'You said that!'

Yes, he did say that.

She is sobbing again, violently, next to the towering snout of a truck. Raindrops hang on it, on horizontals of metal and plastic. He sees them, hanging there. They shake, and some of them fall, as a moment of fierce wind hits everything. Some of them fall. Some of them don't. They hold on, shaking. He says, loosening his hold on her shaking arm, just wanting to end this awful episode among the trucks, 'I'm sorry. I'm sorry I said that.'

It seems so smooth, the way it moves on the endless tarmac. Whispering wheels. It is quiet. No one seems to have anything to say. Not even the weather now. For some kilometres a light mist comes off the motorway, and then it is just blandly dry.

Pearl-grey afternoon.

At Mainz, they cross the Rhine.

He knows Mainz as the city where Gutenberg invented printing, and thus ended the Middle Ages; that was what they decided, anyway, at a seminar he attended at the University of Bologna some years ago, 'The Middle Ages: Approaching the Question of a Terminal Date'. He was asked, afterwards, to write an introduction to their transcripted proceedings.

He finds himself thinking about that, about the terminal date of the Middle Ages, as they pass across the Weisenauer Rheinbrücke, the water on either side a sluggish khaki.

Modernity was what happened next.

Modernity, which has never much interested him. Modernity, what's happening now.

It started here in Mainz.

And the Roman Empire ended here – from here the legions tried to outstare the tribes on the other side of the demarcating waterway, where now there is the Opel factory at Rüsselsheim, and a little further on Frankfurt airport, the actual airport, an enormity flanking the motorway for five whole minutes.

And the weather darkens again as they leave the airport behind.

What has been said in the last hour?

Nothing.

Nothing has been said.

Pine forests on hillsides start to envelop them on the east side of the Main. And fog.

Nel mezzo del cammin di nostra vita

Mi ritrovai per una selva oscura

Well, here it is. Dark pine forests, hemming the motorway. Shapes of fog throw themselves at the windscreen.

Finally someone speaks. He says, 'When did you find out?'

'A few days ago,' she says. 'I didn't want to tell you on the phone.'

'No.'

A few more minutes, and then he says, 'And is it mine? Are you sure it's mine? I have to ask.'

She says nothing.

'Well I just don't know, do I?' he says.

Sex happens, surprisingly, at the Gasthaus Sonne in Trennfeld. It's what they always do – hurry to the hired space to undress. It's what they always do, and they do it now out of habit, not knowing what else to do when they are alone in the hotel room. This time, however, he makes no effort to please her. He wants her to dislike him. If she decides she dislikes him, he thinks, she may decide that she does not want this pregnancy. He is hurried, forceful, almost violent. And when she is in tears afterwards, he feels awful and sits on the toilet with his head in his hands.

It took them an hour to find Trennfeld in the fog – a village of tall half-timbered houses on a steep bluff above the Main. Every second house with a sign saying ZIMMER FREI. A few more formal inns – with parking space in front and paths down to the river at the back – in one of which they have a room.

He had told her, as they picked their way through the fog, that she should not assume, should she decide to keep this child, that it would mean they would stay together. It would not necessarily mean that. Not at all. It was only fair, he said, that he should tell her that.

She said nothing.

She had said little or nothing for the last two hours.

Then she said, 'You don't understand.'

Sliding across a mysterious foggy junction, he said, 'What don't I understand?'

'That I love you,' she said drily.

Well she would say that, he thought, *wouldn't she*. Still, his hands took a firmer hold on the wheel.

A sign at the roadside told them, then, that they had arrived at Trennfeld.

And there it was, the picturesque street of half-timbered houses. The Gasthaus Sonne. The low-beamed reception area. The narrow stairs with the Internet router flickering on the wall, up which the smiling Frau led them to their room.

She had a shower and found him lying on the bed, on the grape-coloured counterpane, waiting for her.

Later, when he emerges from the bathroom's rose-tiled box, she is still crying. Naked except for the coverlet that she has pulled partially over her. 'I'm sorry,' he says, sitting down on the edge of the bed. It did not sound very sincere so he says it again. 'I'm sorry.'

'It's just,' he says, 'this is such a shock. To me.'

'You don't think it's a shock to me?' There is a pillow over her head. Her voice is muffled, tear-clogged, defiant.

He looks from her pale shoulders to the insipid watercolour on the orange wall.

'Of course it is,' he says. 'That's why we need to think about this. We need to think about it seriously. I mean . . .' He wonders how to put this. 'You need to think about *your* life. About what you want from it.'

He knows she is ambitious. She is a TV journalist – pops up on the local Kraków news interviewing farmers about the drought, or the mayor of some nearby town about his new leisure centre and how he managed to snare matching funds from the European Union. She is only twenty-five, and she is almost famous, in the Kraków area. (She probably makes more money than he does, now he thinks about it.) People say hello to her in the street sometimes, point to her on the shopping centre escalator. He was there when that happened. He enjoyed it. They were going down and someone on the way up pointed her out to the people they were with. He had put his hands on her shoulders – he was standing on the step above her – and said, 'What was that about? You're famous?'

'No,' she laughed. 'Not really.'

She is though, and she wants more. He knows that.

'Do you see what I'm saying?' he asks.

They spend a few hours in the dim, curtained room as the afternoon wears on. Nothing outside the room, on the other side of the crimson curtains, which glow dully with the daylight pressing on them from without, seems to have any significance. The room itself seems pregnant, swollen with futures in the blood-dim light.

And the light persists. It is high summer. The evenings last forever. Finally, as if outstared by the sun, they dress and leave.

Outside it is warm and humid. They start to walk up the picturesque half-timbered street. There are some other people around, people strolling in the evening, and on the terraces of the two or three inns, people.

She has said nothing. He feels, however, he feels more and more, that when she thinks about the situation she will see that it would not be sensible to keep it. It would just not be *sensible*. And she *is* sensible. He knows that about her. She is not sentimental. She takes her own life seriously. Has plans for herself, is successfully putting them in train. It is one of the things he likes about her.

He notices that there are cigarette vending machines, several of them, in the street, out in the open. They look strange among the fairy-tale houses. A village of neurotic smokers. He would like to have a cigarette himself. Sometimes, *in extremis*, he still smokes.

Nothing seems very solid, and in fact there is a mist, nearly imperceptible, hanging in the street as the warm evening sucks the moisture out of the wet earth.

They sit down at a table on one of the terraces.

He wonders what to talk about. Should he just talk about anything? About this pretty place? About the high steep roofs of the houses? About the carved gables? About the long day he has had? About what they might do tomorrow?

None of these subjects seem to have any significance. And on the one subject that does seem to have significance, he feels he has said everything there is to say. He does not want to say it all again. He does not want her to feel that he is pressuring her.

It is very important, he thinks, that the decision should be hers, that she should *feel* it was hers.

They sit in silence for a while, surrounded by soft German voices. Older people, mostly, in this place. Older people on their summer holidays.

He says, desperate to know, 'What are you thinking?'

'Why did you choose this place?'

'Why?' He is not prepared for the simple, ordinary question. 'It wasn't too far from the airport,' he says. 'I didn't want to drive too much farther today. It was in the direction we were going in. The hotel looked OK. That's all. It's OK, isn't it?'

'It's fine,' she says.

He turns his head to take in part of the street and says, 'It's not very interesting, I know.'

'That's why I like it.' They share that too – an interest in uninteresting places.

'I wouldn't like to stay here for a week or something,' he says.

'No,' she agrees.

Though after all, why not? He does find a lot to like in this place. It is tidy. Quietly prosperous. Secluded in its modestly hilly landscape. Evidently, not much ever happens. There aren't even any shops – or perhaps there is one somewhere, one that is open mornings only, on weekdays (except Wednesday). Hence, presumably, the cigarette machines. Maybe, with a teaching post at the Universität Würzburg, twenty minutes up the motorway, he would be able to find a way of living here . . .

As a train of thought it is absurd.

And escapist, in its own weird way.

A weird escapist fantasy, is what it is.

A fantasy of hiding himself in a place where nothing ever happens.

She has another taste of her peach juice. She is drinking peach juice, though that does not necessarily mean anything – she is not a habitual drinker.

'And now,' she says, 'we'll never forget it.'

The noises around them seem to slide away to the edges of a tight, soundless space. He hears his own voice saying, 'Why will we never forget it?', as if it wasn't obvious what she meant. And when she says nothing, he wonders, fighting down a wave of panic, *Is this her way of telling me?*

He does not want her to feel that he is pressuring her.

Panicking, he says, 'Please don't make a decision now that you'll wish later you hadn't made.'

'I won't,' she says.

They sit there, swifts shrieking in the hot white sky.

'Just,' he says. 'Please. You know what I think. I won't say it all again.'

And then a minute later, he is saying it all again, everything he said in the hotel.

About how they don't know each other that well.

About the impact it will have on her life. On their life together.

There is a furtive desperation in his eyes.

'Stop this *please*,' she says, turning away in her sunglasses. 'Stop it.'

'I'm sorry . . .'

She starts to well up again; a solitary tear plummets down her face.

'I'm sorry,' he says again, embarrassed. People are starting to look at them.

He has, he thinks, really fucked this up now. His hand moves to take hers, then stops.

He feels as if his surface has been stripped, like a layer of paint, all the underlying terrors exposed.

'I just need to know,' he says.

'*What* do you need to know?'

It seems obvious. 'What's going to *happen*?'

'What you want to happen,' she says.

'It's not what *I* want . . .'

'Yes it is.'

'I don't want you to do it just because *I* want it . . .'

'I'm *not* doing it just because *you* want it.'

It is like waking up from a nightmare, to find your life still there, as you left it. The sounds of the world, too, are there again. It is as if his ears have popped. 'OK,' he says, now taking her hand. 'OK.' It would not do to seem too happy. And in fact, to his surprise, there is a trace of sadness now, somewhere inside him – a sort of vapour trail of sadness on the otherwise blue sky of his mind.

She sobs for a minute or two, quietly, while he holds her hand and tries to ignore the looks of the pensioners who are watching them now without pretence, as if, in this place where nothing ever happens, they were a piece of street theatre.

Which they aren't.

3

The motorway is taking them north-east, towards Dresden. In the vicinity of each town the traffic thickens. The sun looks down at it all, at the hurrying traffic glittering on the motorways of Germany. It is Monday.

They woke late, to find the sun beating at the curtains, beating to be let in. Heat throbbed from the sun-beaten curtains. They had kicked off the bedding. She had not slept well. She was, in some sense, it seemed to him, in mourning. He had no intention of talking about it, not today.

Last night, after the scene on the terrace, they had walked for an hour, walked to the end of the village and then along the river – little paths led down to it, to wooden jetties where boats were tied in the green water. Steep banks on the other side, where there were more pretty houses. Clouds of gnats floated over the water. It was evening, then, finally. Dusk.

They walked back to the Gasthaus Sonne. They hadn't eaten anything.

In the harshly lit room, she said, 'You always get what you want. I know that.'

'That isn't true,' he murmured. Though even then he thought, *Maybe it is. Maybe I do.*

She was undressing. 'I should get used to that,' she said. 'I know people like you.'

'Meaning?'

'People that just drift through life, always getting what they want.' She was speaking quietly, not looking at him, undressing.

'You don't know me,' he told her.

'I know you well enough,' she said.

'Well enough for what?'

She went into the bathroom with her washbag.

He lay down on the soft mattress. He was still trying to think of a single significant instance, in his whole life, when he did not get what he wanted. The fact was, his life was exactly how he wanted it to be.

It had been his plan to visit Bamberg the next morning, and that is what they did. They stuck to his plan, and spent the morning sightseeing, as if nothing had happened. In the Romanesque simplicity of the cathedral, he pored over the tombs of Holy Roman Emperors.

HEINRICH II, † 1024

The Middle Ages. Yesterday's mad scenes next to the motorway, among the trucks, seemed very far away in the limpid atmosphere of the nave. Their feet whispered on the stone floor. They were walking together, looking at statues. He felt safe there, doing that. He did not want to leave, to step out of the hush into the sun, the blinding white square.

She still wasn't saying much. She had hardly spoken to him all morning.

Maybe this *was* the end, he thought, as they walked in the streets of Bamberg, every blue shadow vibrating with detail.

Maybe she had decided – as he had intended, in the madness of yesterday – that she didn't like him.

He had disappointed her, there was no doubt about that.

Lunch, though, was almost normal.

Sunlight fell through leaves into the quiet garden where waiters moved among the tables. *This* was what he had imagined. This was what he had had in mind. Not the scenes next to the motorway. This windless walled garden, the still shadows of these leaves. This was what he wanted.

That she is pregnant, and what will happen about that, is the one thing he does not want to talk about. The decision has been made.

There is nothing else to say. They will, at some point, have to discuss practicalities. Doctors. Money. Until then, talking about it might simply open it up again – might somehow unmake the decision – so he stays away from the subject, or anything like it.

And then the disturbing little moment at the church of the Vierzehnheiligen.

After lunch they drove out of the town to the church of the Vierzehnheiligen. They were standing outside the church, and he was reading from a pamphlet they had picked up at one of the tourist stands. There were lots of people about – coachloads of people walking up from the car park. Sun hats and little battery-powered fans. 'On the twenty-fourth of September 1445,' he read, 'Hermann Leicht, the young shepherd of a nearby Franciscan monastery, saw . . .'

He stopped.

He would not have started if he had known how the story went.

He went on, quickly, 'A crying child in a field that belonged to the nearby Cistercian monastery of Langheim. As he bent down to pick up the child . . .'

He had already started on the next sentence when he saw, with a wave of something like mild nausea, that it was even worse.

'As he bent down to pick up the child, it abruptly disappeared.'

He wondered whether to stop reading the thing out.

Deciding that that would only make matters worse, he went on, speaking quickly. 'A short time later, the child reappeared in the same spot. This time, two candles were burning next to it. In June 1446, Leicht saw the child for a third time. This time, the child was accompanied by thirteen other children, and said: "We are the fourteen helpers and wish to erect a chapel here, where we can rest. If you will be our servant, we will be yours!" It is alleged that miraculous healings soon began, through the intervention of the fourteen saints. That's it,' he said, eager to move on. He shoved the pamphlet into his pocket. 'Should we go in?'

They went in.

And then inside, in the mad marble dream of the interior, something similar happened.

They were standing at the altar, inspecting the statuary there; he was referring to a slip of paper he had picked up near the entrance that had a schematic representation of it – each statue was numbered and there was a key to indentify them. That was what he was doing. Pointing to each of the fourteen helpers, and telling her who they were, and how they helped. For instance, he pointed to one and said, 'St Agathius, invoked against headache.' Or, 'St Catherine of Alexandria, invoked against sudden death.' Or, 'St Margaret of Antioch, invoked in . . .'

It was too late – he had to say it.

'Childbirth.'

He wished then more than ever that they had not driven out there, in the heat of the day. He didn't like baroque, or whatever this was. And he had a feeling that something was coming unstuck.

The next saint, he told her, was St Vitus, invoked against epilepsy.

'St Vitus's dance. And so on,' he said. Her eyes, he was sure, were still on St Margaret of Antioch. 'Here, I won't read them all.' He handed her the paper and, after standing there for a few seconds, started off at a leisurely pace across the brown marble floor, past pinkish columns, their markings swirling like the clouds of Jupiter.

She was still at the altar.

The place was as full as a station at rush hour.

Full of murmurous voices like the wind in a forest.

He found himself standing in front of the font – another extraordinary accretion of kitsch – staring at its pinks, its golds, its powder blues.

A stone bishop holding in his hands his own gold-hatted head.

As weird, he thought, as anything in any Inca or Hindu house of worship.

A stone bishop holding in his hands his own gold-hatted head.

A martyr. Presumably. And he wondered, with the habit of

wanting to know, who this man was. This man, who had invited oblivion on himself, or taken it peaceably – the stone face on the severed head was nothing if not peaceful – when it took him.

Oblivion.

He looked up, looked for her where she had been, at the altar.

Not there.

His eyes found her nearer the entrance, where the devotional candles were. And she had put a euro in the box and was taking a candle and lighting it from one of the ones already there.

He wondered, again, whether she was in any sense devout. Her personal mores – as far as he had been able to make them out – suggested not. Or at least had not in any way led him to think that she might be. The first time he had set eyes on her, more or less, she had been snorting cocaine, at Mani's party.

Everyone else in that space was moving, it seemed, and she was standing still. She was standing still and watching the little flame she had lit.

Which meant what?

He wanted to ask her. He did not dare. He was frightened about what she might say.

'I preferred the cathedral in Bamberg,' he said, as they walked down the hill, hoping that she would agree – as if *that* would mean anything. As if it would dispel the worries that had started, since they arrived at this place, to interfere with his tranquillity.

She said she would have expected him to prefer the cathedral. 'You're not interested in anything post about 1500,' she said, 'are you?'

'1500,' he said, pleased that she was at least being flippant, 'at the very latest.'

'Why is that, do you think?'

'I don't know.'

'You must have some idea. You must have thought about it.'

'It's just an aesthetic preference.'

'Is it?' She was sceptical.

'I think so. I just feel no love,' he said, 'for a place like that.' He meant the Vierzehnheiligen, and he seemed determined to do it down.

When she started to praise the tumbling fecundity of its decoration, he took it almost personally.

'I just don't like it,' he said. 'OK?'

She laughed. 'OK. Fine.'

'I'm sorry. Whatever. You liked it. I didn't. Fine.'

They drove back to the motorway – a few kilometres through humid fields of yellow rapeseed.

'Why did you light that candle?' he asked, trying to sound no more than vaguely interested.

'I don't know.'

'I didn't know you were religious,' he said.

'I'm not.'

'So?'

'I just felt like it. Is it a problem?'

'Of course not. I was wondering, that's all.'

'I just felt like it,' she said again.

He asked, 'You don't believe in God?'

'I don't know. No. Do you?'

He laughed as if it should be obvious. 'No. Not even slightly.'

And then they were on the motorway again, north-east, towards Dresden.

He said, after a while, 'I'll pay for it of course. The . . .' He tried to find a neutral word. 'Procedure.'

He needed to know that the decision still stood.

It seemed it did.

She said, just looking levelly out at the motorway, 'OK.' And then, 'Thank you.'

'Of course.'

He wondered, having started to talk about it, whether to talk about it some more. To ask, for instance, *where* she wanted to have it done. The procedure. To nail it down with details. Specific places. Times.

The silence, while he wondered this, ended up lasting for over an hour.

And now they are stuck in a traffic jam outside Dresden. It is five in the afternoon. Light screams off windscreens. The air conditioning pours frigid air over them.

Satisfied again that he has no major problem, small ones start to trouble him. It was a fault in his plan for today, he thinks, that they should be passing Dresden at this time. He ought to have known that this would happen. It was foreseeable. (He moves forward another few metres, sick of the sight of the van in front of him. A scruffy white van. Ukrainian plates.) It was an unforced error.

And the damage to Stańko's paintwork, the unspeakable scuff – yes, that is still there, to be dealt with, to be talked about, to be apologised for.

To be paid for.

Another thing to be paid for.

4

He is thinking about the piece he needs to write for the *Journal of English and Germanic Philology*. 'Anomalous Factors in the Form "Slēan" – Some Suggestions'. He is in the shower, offering his face to the warm streams of water, thinking about it. Thinking about the work that needs to be done. The hours that will need to be spent in libraries – Oxford, London, Paris, Heidelberg. The shower is in a sort of hollow in a stone wall – the whole bathroom is like that. The windows, two of them, are narrow slits. The functional elements, though, are impeccably modern. The tiles on the floor are warm to the soles of his feet when he steps out of the shower and takes a heavy towel. Tastefully done, everything. Once it was a monastery, now it is an upmarket hotel. While he towels himself he leans towards one of the windows, which is set in a deep narrowing slot in the wall, to see out – steep forested hills, quite far away. He likes to imagine the time when this *was* a monastery, when it sat in fields next to the meandering, pristine waters of the Elbe. When the only way to get to Königstein was by walking for an hour. When Dresden was a whole day's walk away. He towels his hair, flattens it with his hand until he is satisfied with how it looks. 'Anomalous Factors in the Form "Slēan" '. That must be his focus now. Now that this nightmare is over, and the future is there again.

It is early evening. The sun puts warm shapes on the wall opposite the windows. The decoration is monastic minimalist: fluid lines, unelaborated. Polished stone. White sheets. Everything white.

She is sitting on a pale leather sofa, hugging her knees, looking towards one of the windows, with its view over neat modern houses to the hills further away. Slightly disappointingly, the hotel is surrounded by suburban normality. Some streets of newish single-family houses, and a sort of industrial estate.

Kilted in the white towel he descends the two stone steps from the shower room. He starts to search in his suitcase for his deodorant. 'Are you hungry?' he asks.

She is sitting on the sofa, hugging her knees.

He applies deodorant.

'Are you hungry?' he asks again, not impatiently, just with a different intonation, as if she might not have heard him the first time, though she must have.

'The food's supposed to be excellent,' he tells her, looking forward to the meal himself. 'French. They've got a Michelin star.'

This was to be their treat, this immaculate hotel and its Michelin-starred food – their indulgence, their luxury. Tomorrow night they will be at her place in Kraków. The day after that, she will be at work again, on television, and he will be on a flight to Stansted. She likes her work. Just after they arrived at the hotel, late this afternoon, someone had phoned her. It turned out to be her producer. It was interesting to hear her work voice, and it had seemed obvious, overhearing her – just from the tone, he understood nothing else – where her priorities were.

He is doing up his linen shirt.

She is sitting on the sofa, hugging her knees.

'I can't do it.'

'Can't do what?' He thinks she might mean the Michelin-starred meal, that she is feeling too depressed or something.

When she doesn't answer him, he starts to see that this is wrong. She does not mean the meal.

'I thought you decided,' he says, quietly, trying to sound unperturbed as he does up his shirt.

'So did I.'

He finishes doing up his shirt. What this means, he thinks, is that he will have to do it all again. He will have to do yesterday evening, again. She is going to make them do that again. He sighs, through his nose. Then he sits down on the pale sofa. She is sitting sideways with her feet on the sofa, facing away from him, and he puts his hands on her shoulders and starts to say, again, all the things he said yesterday.

'I know,' she says.

He is saying the things, softly saying them, with a tired voice, as if he is unpacking them, and putting them out on a table for her to see.

'I know,' she says.

He is whispering them in her ear, his mouth is next to her ear. He is able to smell the light scent of her sweat – fresh sweat and stale sweat. To feel on his face, which sometimes touches hers, the dampness of her tears.

'I know,' she says, 'I know.'

His arms are encircling her, his hands on her stomach.

'It's all true what you're saying,' she says.

'Yes, it is . . .'

'And none of it makes any difference. I just can't.'

She takes his hands in her hands. Other than that, she does not move. Her hands are very warm and very damp.

She says, 'This child has chosen me to be its mother, and . . . and I just can't turn it away. Please understand.

'Karel,' she says, 'please understand.'

His forehead is heavy on her shoulder. He has tears in his own eyes now and they are wetting the cotton of her shirt.

'Do you understand?' she wants to know, in a whisper.

'No,' he says. It is not quite true. Not quite.

The situation, anyway, is simpler than he thought. It was always very simple. The last two days have been a sort of illusion. There was only ever one possible outcome. He sees that now.

They stay there for a long time, on the pale sofa.

The sun won't stop shining.

'Now what?' he says finally. What he means is: where does this leave us? Where does this leave our two lives?

'Are you hungry?' she asks.

'No,' he immediately says. He finds it hard to imagine ever feeling hunger again. He finds it hard to imagine anything. The future, again, seems no longer to be there.

'Do you want to go for a walk?' she asks, for the first time shifting her position, turning slightly towards him, so that her shoulder moves, and he has to lift his head. 'Let's go for a walk,' she says.

'Where?' Having lifted his head, he is looking at the elegantly minimalist room as if he does not know where he is.

'I don't know,' she says. 'Wherever. Why don't you put some trousers on?'

Docilely, he does.

They leave the hotel and start to walk towards Königstein. The pavement follows the main road. Traffic sometimes whizzes past. Sometimes there is silence, or a hazy noise of insects. Sometimes there are trees, or from somewhere the smell of cut grass.

It is five kilometres to Königstein, the sign says. They do not stop. It is high summer. The light will last for hours. They have time to walk it, if they want to. ■

MAUREEN N. McLANE

Come Again/Woods

They party in the woods
as if they were meant for pleasure
not timber.

Cuts heal.
Second growth.

As if this world
were made for us.
Some think so.

'People piss me off
specifically and species-wise.'

Oh well.

The beer bottle
on the abandoned foundations
of a cabin. Civilization.

Mangy teenagers
acid rain and a sunset.
Who's done with 'nature'?

That old sun
just now
blew me away.

Plant the tree
that your great
grandchildren
will swing from.

Trees for Cities

© HANNAH WHITAKER
Barcroft (Taeuber-Arp), 2014

TO THE OCEAN

Deb Olin Unferth

At the desk they said they encouraged guests not to walk, but she was determined. She took the useless map and they set out, she and her husband, following the boardwalk. When the boardwalk ended they followed the path, she saying the whole way, 'Of course we can walk. Why don't they want us to walk!' until the path ended and they stepped out onto a field, which she determined was a golf course. They hiked across that – 'Bourgeois assholes,' she was saying, marching along, swinging her arms. Her husband kept saying, 'Oh, here's where it ends,' and 'I don't think we're allowed in there,' and 'I'm not walking in that,' while she thought, If I had married someone else, it wouldn't be like this. She thought longingly of a man she might have married, blurry, nondescript, one who no doubt would be laughing and running up the hills. This, while her sister sent a text, 'Where are you? We took the shuttle. We've been here half an hour.'

Later at the picnic her husband would describe it to the sister, who'd be laughing. 'Oh I can see it!' the sister would say. 'I can see her coming down the side of the mountain, struggling through the trees, bruised and bleeding.' 'There she goes!' her husband would say about her imaginary figure cutting through the brush. And the sister and husband would both continue to tease her throughout the day, provide running commentary on her actions. 'Making sandwiches for the revolution,' they'd say. 'Pouring coffee for the revolution. Having a swim for the revolution.'

Before all that, while they were still on their way, she and her husband came to the edge of the golf course and looked out over the cliffs and beyond, the first glimpse of their destination – the water, hazy and distant. There was so much to get through between here and there: trees, a whole forest of them, the downside of a steep mountain, tall grasses, weeds to your hips, misunderstandings, ticks and mosquitoes and spiders and other disappointments, lost jobs, lost faculties, dying parents and so much more. 'Don't,' he said, but she would do it. She steadied herself to walk in. ∎

Hunters in the Snow

The hunters have all failed,
the three hunters and their forlorn dogs
now arriving home from the mountain
which thunders above their village
with nothing to show for their expedition
except one dead fox.

Nobody has noticed yet:

not the crones attending their stringy fire,

not the families skating or playing hurly
on two square ponds among several
that fill the flat-bottomed valley.

Perhaps that large black bird – a crow
with a tail as long as a phoenix
sailing from its bare tree –
is paying attention.
If so, the friends he has left song-less
and frozen among their branches
show no appetite to follow suit.

One advantage the hunters still have
is the high ground that allows them a view
of the whole world as they know it,
and its population like dust-spots
darkening a smoky mirror.

This might well lead them to decide
they have the perspective of gods,
and have arrived here as men
who understand the future
and know it shares their wretchedness,
their dearth of any good things.

They might be planning in fact
to make everyone else in their image,
including the miller
who now appears beside his frozen wheel
and rhythmically claps his hands
in time with a song that has lasted for generations,
saying Winter will end in a trice, fol-de-rol,
and water will shortly run in its channels again.

But nothing like this will ever happen.
Their slow tramp and miserably lowered gaze
means they do not know their advantage.

Therefore they keep walking.
They do not speak.
They ignore their dogs.
And in a moment will pass from the bare trees
and flare of the firelight
and so make their descent,
with each in his own way
thinking it is enough to live
as nothing except himself.

To find sufficient beauty
in hearing their footsteps creak
when they approach the threshold
and break its crust of frozen snow.

Granta 135:
New Irish Writing

A century ago the Irish took up arms to end British rule –
the Easter Rising marked the beginning of a period of drastic
social and political changes that continue to reverberate through
Irish life.

Aesthetically, too, it has been a century of great experimentation,
exploration and evolution. *Granta* 135: New Irish Writing
celebrates one of the most distinguished literary traditions from
a contemporary perspective, showcasing new work from up-and-
coming talent as well as from the country's most established voices.

An issue of fiction, memoir, reportage, poetry, photography
and art, New Irish Writing will chart the many places, identities
and stories that make up a nation.

FRAGMENTS

Roger Deakin

Introduction by Robert Macfarlane

In 1969 Roger Deakin bought a ruined farmhouse in Mellis, a small village in north Suffolk. Walnut Tree Farm sat on the edge of Mellis Common, a medieval grazing pasture that centuries of farming had made rich with wild flowers, including rare green-winged orchids and sulphur clover. Over the course of several years, Roger rebuilt the farmhouse – first raised in the Elizabethan era – according to a traditional East Anglian method of timber-framing that allowed the house to sit upon the shifting clays of Suffolk and flex in response to the earth's own flexes. At the back of the house was a spring-fed moat in which Roger would swim, twelve acres of meadow and more than half a mile of hedgerows. Along one side of his land ran the Ipswich–Norwich railway line, and perpendicular to the railway was an ancient right of way known as Cowpasture Lane.

Roger lived at Walnut Tree Farm for thirty-seven years, until his untimely death in the summer of 2006. Though he travelled widely and often, he always returned: it was, he wrote, his 'den', his 'sett'. Living there as long as he did, he came to know the habits, the weather and the creatures of his landscape intimately. Roger was a self-taught naturalist and over the decades he recorded his observations of life at Walnut Tree Farm in dozens of notebooks and journals, mostly Moleskines, which he filled with his spidery black handwriting.

Thinking of Roger in Mellis, I am often put in mind of Henry David Thoreau in Walden. Both men were journal-keepers, both were naturalists and phenologists, both lived by water, both loved trees and woods, and the landscape of Walden – like that of Mellis – was bounded on one side by a railway line, such that both men could hear the rattle of freight trains passing in the night. But Thoreau only lived by Walden Pond for two years, whereas Roger was in Mellis for almost four decades. The result of his chronic acquaintance with that place was a fabulously deep knowing, made subtle by the long view as well as the close-up.

Two years after Roger's death, Terence Blacker and Alison Hastie edited a selection of his notebooks, which were subsequently published as *Notes from Walnut Tree Farm* in 2008. That much-loved book soon became a classic of English localism, part of a tradition that stretches back to diarists and journal-keepers such as Francis Kilvert and Gilbert White. It also completed a loose trilogy of Roger's books, along with *Waterlog* (1999) and *Wildwood* (2007).

A year later, Roger's archive was acquired by the University of East Anglia, which catalogued and organised his thousands of papers, files, cassettes and notebooks, and made them available to researchers and readers. What follows is a series of previously unpublished fragments from Roger's work at Walnut Tree Farm, selected from the archive by Luke Neima and arranged seasonally. They offer glimpses through the remarkable eyes of the man who lived for so long in this remarkable landscape.

Spring

There's a great spring-cleaning wind blowing away the dross of winter and ushering in the beginning of spring from the west. By the time it reaches Suffolk, the west wind has warmed itself over the Atlantic, then picked up all the scents of hazel catkins on the Burren, heather on Dartmoor and Exmoor, and the lichened oak woods of Wales, before flowing across Suffolk and the open Brecklands bending the reed tops on the fens and snapping my old maple tree off its westernmost roots, half severed by a digger in the ditch last year.

Yesterday the ash arch began to come into leaf, just sprouting at the tips of the laid horizontal branches at first, and then a few flowers. Wild hops suddenly leaping and grappling up the grey, smooth ladies' stockings ash bark. The quince and cow parsley and ash blossom/ leaf all began on the same day, when the wind went round and four swallows appeared. They flew over the house and then turned left and disappeared somewhere else. How I longed for them to stop here instead. They took a turn or two overhead, then just went. To Monks Hall in Syleham, perhaps. A moorhen is sitting on a nest in the front moat, too. Ash seedlings are coming through, and maple. Mistletoe and the kisses allowed beneath it, so long as it has berries. The white, the green and the gold of the plant and its legendary hardwood (it was once used to make spears). The only tree to leaf in midwinter and therefore magical. Kisses were forbidden at all other seasons except the anarchic, rambunctious Saturnalia.

The three woods are all very different. Stubbing's is yellow with primroses, Gipping is pale pink white with wood anemones, or dark green with the shining leaves of ramsons, or snaked about with the blotched leaves of early purple orchids. Burgate is surprisingly bare of flowers, except in a few particular places, where there are beds of primroses or a tiny patch of lungwort or another tiny patch of herb Paris and early purple orchids.

We live in symbiotic association with trees – they are an intimate part of all our lives. We eat of them, open and shut them to go in and out of our houses and bedrooms. We play cricket with them, we sail the seas with them and row boat races with them. We eat our daily bread on them, we warm ourselves before them at the hearth, we sit on them, play croquet with them, canoe rivers in them, grow runner beans up them, build sheds and shacks out of them, sit underneath their shade in summer, reading books or picnicking, read them every morning on the train to work or borrow them from the library.

The roots of trees are a great mystery. Some, like the fig and the eucalyptus, are capable of putting down phenomenally deep systems. Somehow, they know the water is there beneath the ground, and they know where it is. How do they know? There's a story of a fig that thrust its roots deep into the ground along the wall of All Souls College in Oxford and a root was found in the wine cellar, growing clean through the cork and into a bottle of vintage port.

Plunging into the cool green depths of a daydream always feels very much the same as swimming out across the dark bed of a wood. The book has leaves, the words are twigs, the trees whisper and breathe, and lovers record their passions in the bark, especially in the smooth bark of the beech, the buche – the book of love.

My sense of loss, of expulsion from paradise, stays with me since my father died when I was seventeen. I think my strong desire to find and buy a ruin – this house – and to repair it, to bring it back to life, to breathe new life into it, has been a way of bringing my father back to life. It is the same with my efforts at conservation, my interest in it. I don't want things to die, to become extinct. I want to breathe new life into things and fight to defend their life.

Summer

A hot day, and I was in and out of the moat five or six times. Cleared some weeds in the boat. Slept in the railway wagon, as I did the night before. Deep, dreaming sleep; again a boat and islands and deep tidal channels somewhere – to the south of Spain, Ibiza or Mallorca. An indeterminate dream-landscape, tentatively trying to sail a boat I'm not fully in command of, which I don't quite understand.

On Thursday, with the heat: a dozen little yellow-striped hoverflies at work on a white umbelliferae flower like a sea; a drunken bee asleep at the wheel on the blue globe of an echinops flower, too drunk with pollen to move.

I go weeding the moat.

Ask yourself unlikely questions about water, come at it from every angle. What lives in it – beneath its surface? Why is water like our own minds? There are the thoughts that flit about on its surface, but the real world of the mind all goes on beneath, in the depths of the unconscious mind, which are like the depths of the ocean. That's the part of us that dreams.

The little purring, soft, bubbling calls of rooks as they fly home together.

I walked down to the railway meadow and surprised a pair of feral cats down there, one black, hunting in the felled rows of cut hay, one white, basking in the sun. I suspect the white one is deaf, as white cats often are, and that it uses the black one as a bodyguard, to warn it of approaching dangers. Both cats raced off into the wood when they noticed me, first the black one, followed by the white.

Out in the flowery hay, the meadow browns floated up wherever I went in their lolling flight, and the little gatekeeper butterflies winked their wings, almost like a chorus of thanks for being left alone.

Yesterday afternoon I picked blackberry in the hedge I laid a few years ago, now billowing back into exuberant life. It is almost September and the south-facing bushes are a glistening black cascade of berries. They come tumbling into the bowl, as full of purple juice as grapes. Earwigs and spiders drop in too, scrambling up the sides to escape and sliding back to be lost again under the mound of nuggets.

Back in the kitchen I dissected one of the best of the fruit, prising off each fruitlet with a pair of tweezers to count them. As I did so, they burst and the juice splashed on the sheet of paper underneath, smudging into a misty purple watercolour of bramble bushes. There were sixty-four fruitlets on both the blackberries I dissected, then I weakened and ate the rest in a bowl with yoghurt.

Wasps and greenbottles crawled about the bramble bush on the fruit and a red admiral sucked in an ecstasy of intoxication completely still, just flexing its wings in pleasure now and then.

I take my rug outside to shake and lay it on the terrace and another red admiral comes and suns itself on the Turkish pattern's butterfly colours.

Autumn

There is always something devotional about lighting a fire; praying it will kindle and take off with its own life. It is a kind of birth since it often requires bellows, there's something musical about it too. And its careful construction twig by twig when the glow comes and the first tiny flames struggle out of the darkness is certainly architecture. It is also physics because you are learning about energy and mass, and their delicate relationship, how one turns into the other, leaving only a warmer room and a little ash to scatter on the roots of the russet-apple tree, or the potato garden.

The hearth is quite obviously the most sacred, numinous place in the house. It lies at its centre, and it is the only part of the house that opens to the skies. Everything in the house points towards it, and everyone is drawn towards its warmth and comfort and above all, fascination. It has a life of its own, it demands to be fed.

Thought I heard something 'ticking' by the desk facing the moat. It is a beetle – small, brown, long-bodied, that seems caught in a spider's web and is 'ticking' with periodic convulsions so that it uncoils like a spring with a 'click'. I also notice a much longer beetle-hole in the beam. Could it be deathwatch? Not sure it is: it's the right size, but doesn't look quite right in colour and is a little too long and thin. Rotten pollard willow tops are deathwatch habitat and they're often brought into the house on firewood. I observe the beetle in a jam jar. I will let it go on a rotten willow in the morning. Half the firewood I bring in to store in the hearth is probably infested with bulbs. I hate the word 'inglenook' – too folksy.

All sorts of things wander in and out of this house. Newts appear late at night, strolling across my study carpet. They seem to know where they're going, and just disappear again if I leave them alone. Sometimes I pick them up and leave them in a flower bed. Toads turn up too, and there's one in residence just outside the door, fooled by the escaping heat into thinking it's spring, and croaking gently all evening. There must be all kinds of cracks and corners creatures can wriggle through, and anyway, the doors stand open most of the summer and autumn, and on sunny days in winter when the wood stove sometimes overheats my study.

The trustful way a moth or dragonfly will cling to your hand, or walk about on it.

There are respectable precedents for spending time observing insects. Nabokov spent years chasing blue butterflies or peering at them through his microscope. It didn't stop him writing. Insects live closer to the land than we do – and the moon and stars too, as far as I can see – responding to nuances in the weather or the lunar calendar, or just a molecule or two of each other's pheromones on the night air, with fanatical fervour.

Our Suffolk common just outside this window, and the four meadows and their hedgerows have been buzzing with insects all spring and summer. Even now, in November, the butterflies keep waking up inside the house and flapping at the window, trailing spiders' webs like bits of torn dress. And ichneumon flies drone loudly round the room as soon as the wood-stove cranks up the temperature past seventy, emerging from the crevices and peg holes in the beams they spent hours sampling on the wing a month or two ago, like divers looking for eels.

A spider's web follows the same plan as a tree trunk. I have counted fifty-nine concentric threads on the spider's web stretched across my windows and measured its diameter as seven inches, although it is more oval than round.

Dolomedes (fimbriatus) carries echoes of Archimedes – also associated in my mind with water, through the famous bath in which he is supposed to have discovered his laws of displacement. The spider relies on another of the laws of physics: surface tension, and the power of the meniscus to buoy up its eight legs spread out across the surface. There's something wise and ancient about spiders too: the feeling that there is a considerable intelligence at work as they watch you.

Entering a wood is to enter an element as different as the sea. The subterranean world of the wood floor, sometimes silent, sometimes noisy with chainsaws and work, full of song, people, clattering axes, human work and the crackling of fire.

The stump of my grandfather's arm where his hand had been amputated looked exactly the same as a tree looks when it heals after a limb has been sawn off. The bark grows together around and over the wound, and it flows towards the centre and meets like water. Grandpa reacted the same way as a tree to the trauma of amputation: he grew up faster and he grew in stature and strength. Plus: he put his roots down deeper. His arm, *sans* hand, looked like a cigar stub.

Winter

One of my greatest pleasures in life is to turn my compost heap. There's a touch of archaeology about it as you peel off successive layers of half-rotted weeds, and something of the quiet satisfaction of counting banknotes. I have my own gang of tiny alchemists, millions of them, all busy turning the dross of old banana skins, potato peel and grass cuttings into the golden, delicious fragrance that will feast this year's salad crop and increase the roses. In winter, you might be stoking a fire, so much steam billows out of the heap, and you can warm your frozen fingers in it. As a vegetable power station, the compost heap is a shanty town for the occasional rat or mouse family, or anything else that likes to keep warm and sheltered. Other people get slow-worms or snakes, but I haven't been so lucky, although I did get a fat, orange-bottomed bumblebee this summer, nesting in the cliff face left by my spade where I quarried.

'Vicious' is the word that springs to mind to describe blackthorn. Call me a masochist or perverse, but I still love these sea urchins of our hedgerows, spiny foot soldiers that will prick you like a wasp or puncture a tractor tyre swifter than a thought. The entire bush is armoured with batteries of hypodermic syringes.

Whenever I've wanted to express what I feel about a particular wood or tree, I have simply gone out and begun some hard physical work with that species, and the wood has never failed to speak to me, to give up its secrets as if they had been withheld to all but the supplicant willing to devote an hour or two of hard labour and expend some effort, even sustain some pain, in the pursuit of the truth about that particular tree. You have to commune with the wood, and to do that you have to work.

Sometimes when I wake up, I see a window or a wall, and wonder, 'Where am I, whose house is this? Which country am I in? Is this a hotel or the bedroom of a friend? A lover?'

Then slowly I remember I am in my own house, and it is just another bedroom. I sleep around, you see, moving from one bedroom to the other, alternating vacant bedrooms or visiting the satellite dens in the fields.

Outside my windows, I hear industrious tapping, like a gardener at work. Is he banging home a fencing post, or mending a gate? It sounds like hammering, and is the vigorous percussion of a thrush's beak and a snail. This thrush is constantly at work at certain particular anvils around the house. One by the pile of peg tiles next to the ash arch, one by the woodshed close to a young walnut tree.

The first thing I see in my window when I wake up is woods. Twelve in one, sixteen in the other – subdivisions of the window. Each frames trees, a lattice of branches, and beyond, a Suffolk sky. Sun just beginning to show from the clouds.

Ash trees kissing and plaiting (maples too) like lovers on the sides of Keats's 'Ode on a Grecian Urn'. 'For ever wilt thou love, and she be fair!' A frozen kiss. The embrace of ivy lianas in the ash leaves an impression, a dent, in the bark. The word is 'ingrained'.

The meandering of a river and the sinuous curving branches of an old coppiced ash are one and the same. They express and map the constant fluctuations in the forces in the world. If an ash tree grows first this way and then that, it is responding to changing conditions of light around it.

I remember studying the leaf and the details of the stomata, cutting delicate sections of leaf with a barber's cut-throat razor, honed on a leather strop at the front of the laboratory classroom. The wonder of stomata. The central political act which our whole future hinges on is that of the exchange of carbon dioxide into and out of the atmosphere, and the release of that element D.H. Lawrence pondered, the very essence of our continued survival: oxygen.

To see each tree as an oxygen factory, and as a trap and reservoir of carbon. So that the best way we can possibly contain and immobilise carbon is to lock it into a tree and utilise that tree as timber and make from it something of lasting beauty. ∎

Ann Beattie's books include the story collections *What Was Mine*, *Follies* and *The New Yorker Stories*, the novel *Chilly Scenes of Winter* and the novella *Walks With Men*. Her most recent collection, *The State We're In: Maine Stories*, was published by Simon & Schuster in the US and is forthcoming from Granta Books in the UK.

Roger Deakin was a writer, film-maker and broadcaster, and the author of *Waterlog* and *Wildwood*. A collection of extracts from his notebooks and journals were published as *Notes from Walnut Tree Farm*, edited by Terence Blacker and Alison Hastie.

Rebecca Giggs writes about ecology and the environmental imagination, animals, landscape, politics and memory. Her essays and stories have appeared in *Best Australian Science Writing*, *Best Australian Stories*, *Aeon*, *Griffith Review* and *Meanjin*. She teaches at Macquarie University in Sydney. Her first book is forthcoming from Scribe.

Kathleen Jamie is a poet and essayist. Her books include the essay collections *Findings* and *Sightlines* and the poetry collections *The Overhaul* and *The Bonniest Companie*, which will be published this autumn. She is Chair of Poetry at Stirling University and lives with her family in Fife.

Noelle Kocot is the author of seven books, including the forthcoming *Phantom Pains of Madness*. She has received numerous honours for her work. She is Poet Laureate of Pemberton, NJ, and teaches writing in New York.

Barry Lopez is the author of fourteen books of fiction and non-fiction, including *Arctic Dreams*, for which he received the 1986 National Book Award.

Robert Macfarlane's books include *Mountains of the Mind*, *The Wild Places*, *The Old Ways* and, most recently, *Landmarks*. He is a Fellow of Emmanuel College, Cambridge, and Roger Deakin's literary executor.

Maureen N. McLane is the author of three poetry collections and of *My Poets*, a hybrid work of memoir and criticism. Her next book of poems, *Mz N: the serial*, comes out in May 2016.

Ben Marcus is the editor of *New American Stories*, published by Vintage in the US and Granta Books in the UK. His most recent books include the novel *The Flame Alphabet* and the story collection *Leaving the Sea*.

Ange Mlinko is the author of *Marvelous Things Overheard*. She is Poetry Editor of the *Nation* and teaches at the University of Florida.

Andrew Motion was the UK's Poet Laureate from 1999 to 2009 and his new collection, *Peace Talks*, is forthcoming by Faber & Faber. He is a Homewood Professor of the Arts at Johns Hopkins University and lives in Baltimore.

Adam Nicolson is the author of several books about history, writing and the environment, including *Sea Room*, *Power and Glory* and *Gentry*. His most recent book is *The Mighty Dead: Why Homer Matters*.

Audrey Niffenegger is a writer and visual artist based in Chicago and London. Her books include *The Time Traveler's Wife*, *Raven Girl* and *Her Fearful Symmetry*. She recently edited and illustrated a collection of ghost stories, *Ghostly*. She has been collecting slightly damaged taxidermy since 1986.

Gus Palmer is a social documentary photographer. He is currently working on a long-term project documenting migration routes into Europe.

Fred Pearce is a freelance author and journalist based in London. He is the environment consultant for *New Scientist*. His books include *The Landgrabbers*, *Confessions of an Eco Sinner* and *The New Wild*.

Helge Skodvin is a Norwegian photographer. His solo show, *A Moveable Beast*, will be presented at the University Museum of Bergen. His first book, *240 Landscapes*, will be published later this year.

David Szalay was one of *Granta*'s Best of Young British Novelists in 2013. He is the author of the novels *London and the South-East*, *The Innocent* and *Spring*. He lives in Budapest.

Deb Olin Unferth is the author of the story collection *Minor Robberies*, the novel *Vacation* and the memoir *Revolution*. Her work has been published in the *New York Times*, *Harper's*, the *Paris Review* and *Granta*.

About the Cover

Stanley Donwood is the pen name of Dan Rickwood, an English artist who has collaborated extensively with Radiohead and whose work has featured on all the band's albums. But to associate Donwood exclusively with Radiohead is to do him – and the breadth and scope of his artistic range – a disservice. In addition to his partnership with Radiohead, Donwood has created artwork for the covers of J.G. Ballard novels and for the Glastonbury festival. He has written and illustrated a number of books and exhibited his work around the world, most recently in Sydney, where a major retrospective was staged in May 2015.

Hurt Hill is taken from a series that was exhibited under the title *Far Away is Close at Hand in Images of Elsewhere*. Other pictures had titles like *Soken Fen, Nether* and *Winterfold*; all culled from Ordnance Survey maps. I'd become interested in what I loosely termed 'the Northern European imagination' and the formulation of fevered myths, legends and folk tales of the dark forests in which we spent so many aeons of ancestral time.

I took myself off to the woods, the fragments of the great forests that once spread over our continent. As dusk creeps through the trees it's easy – very easy – to imagine every ghoul, sprite, elf or pixie that has ever haunted the Northern European mind. Our love of nature, and of all things natural, intensified with industrialisation and the depletion of what we now call 'natural resources'. But it's difficult to feel that love when you are lost as night is falling, walking faster and faster through the forest. My loudest thoughts passing through my mind as I stumbled around in the dark were: 'What's that? What's that? What was that?' ∎

Stanley Donwood